D0566747

THE CLONE WARS™

THE SITH HUNTERS

DESIGNER **KRYSTAL HENNES**

ASSISTANT EDITOR **FREDDYE LINS**

EDITOR **RANDY STRADLEY**

PUBLISHER **MIKE RICHARDSON**

Special thanks to Joanne Chan Taylor, Leland Chee, Troy Alders, Carol Roeder, Jann Moorhead, and David Anderman at Lucas Licensing.

Published by Dark Horse Books, a division of Dark Horse Comics, Inc.
10956 SE Main Street, Milwaukie, OR 97222

DarkHorse.com | StarWars.com

To find a comics shop in your area, call the Comic Shop Locator Service toll-free at 1.888.266.4226
First edition: August 2012 | ISBN 978-1-59582-949-8

10 9 8 7 6 5 4 3 2 1

PRINTED AT 1010 PRINTING INTERNATIONAL, LTD., GUANGDONG PROVINCE, CHINA

Library of Congress Cataloging-in-Publication Data

Gilroy, Henry.
Star wars the clone wars : the Sith hunters / script, Henry Gilroy, Steven Melching ; pencils, Vicenc Villagrasa ; inks, Vicente Ibanez ; lettering, Michael Heisler ; cover art, Dave Filoni.
    p. cm.
Summary: "Darth Maul and his brother Savage Opress are loose in the galaxy. The Jedi Council sends a task force of Jedi to bring them to justice"--Provided by publisher.
ISBN 978-1-59582-949-8
1. Graphic novels. I. Melching, Steven. II. Filoni, Dave, ill. III. Star wars, the clone wars (Television program) IV. Title. V. Title: Sith hunters.
PZ7.7.G55Stm 2012
741.5'973--dc23

2012015596

STAR WARS: THE CLONE WARS—THE SITH HUNTERS
Star Wars © 2012 Lucasfilm Ltd. & ™. All rights reserved. Used under authorization. Text and illustrations for Star Wars are © 2012 Lucasfilm Ltd. Dark Horse Books® and the Dark Horse logo are registered trademarks of Dark Horse Comics, Inc. All rights reserved. No portion of this publication may be reproduced or transmitted, in any form or by any means, without the express written permission of Dark Horse Comics, Inc. Names, characters, places, and incidents featured in this publication either are the product of the author's imagination or are used fictitiously. Any resemblance to actual persons (living or dead), events, institutions, or locales, without satiric intent, is coincidental.

STAR WARS®

THE CLONE WARS™

THE SITH HUNTERS

SCRIPT **HENRY GILROY**
STEVEN MELCHING

PENCILS **VICENÇ VILLAGRASA**

INKS **VICENTE IBAÑEZ**

COLORS **MARLON ILAGAN**

LETTERING **MICHAEL HEISLER**

COVER ART **DAVE FILONI**

DARK HORSE BOOKS

LUCAS BOOKS

This story takes place shortly after the events in "Revenge," episode 22 of season 4 of *The Clone Wars*.

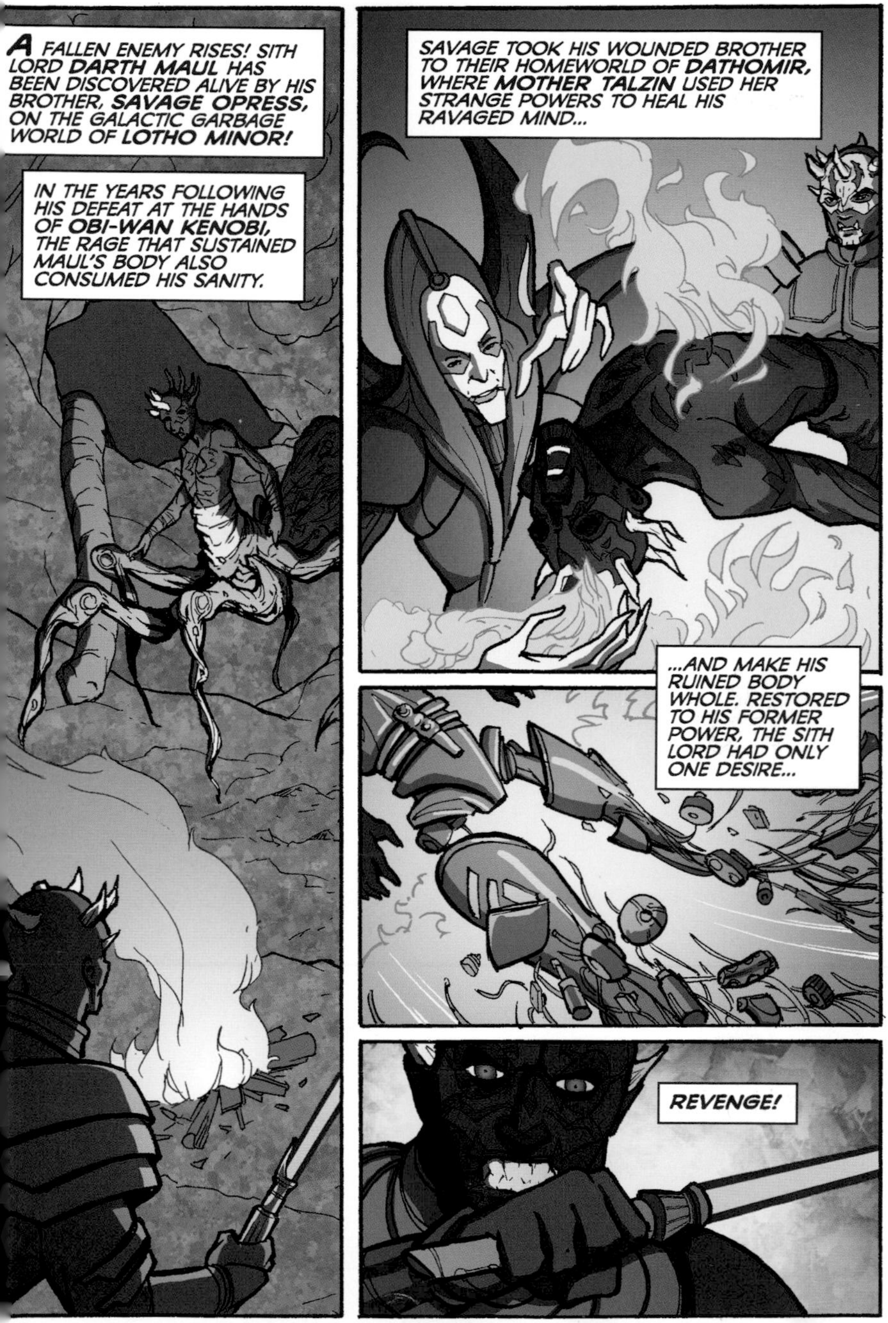
A FALLEN ENEMY RISES! SITH LORD DARTH MAUL HAS BEEN DISCOVERED ALIVE BY HIS BROTHER, SAVAGE OPRESS, ON THE GALACTIC GARBAGE WORLD OF LOTHO MINOR!
IN THE YEARS FOLLOWING HIS DEFEAT AT THE HANDS OF OBI-WAN KENOBI, THE RAGE THAT SUSTAINED MAUL'S BODY ALSO CONSUMED HIS SANITY.
SAVAGE TOOK HIS WOUNDED BROTHER TO THEIR HOMEWORLD OF DATHOMIR, WHERE MOTHER TALZIN USED HER STRANGE POWERS TO HEAL HIS RAVAGED MIND...
...AND MAKE HIS RUINED BODY WHOLE. RESTORED TO HIS FORMER POWER, THE SITH LORD HAD ONLY ONE DESIRE...
REVENGE!

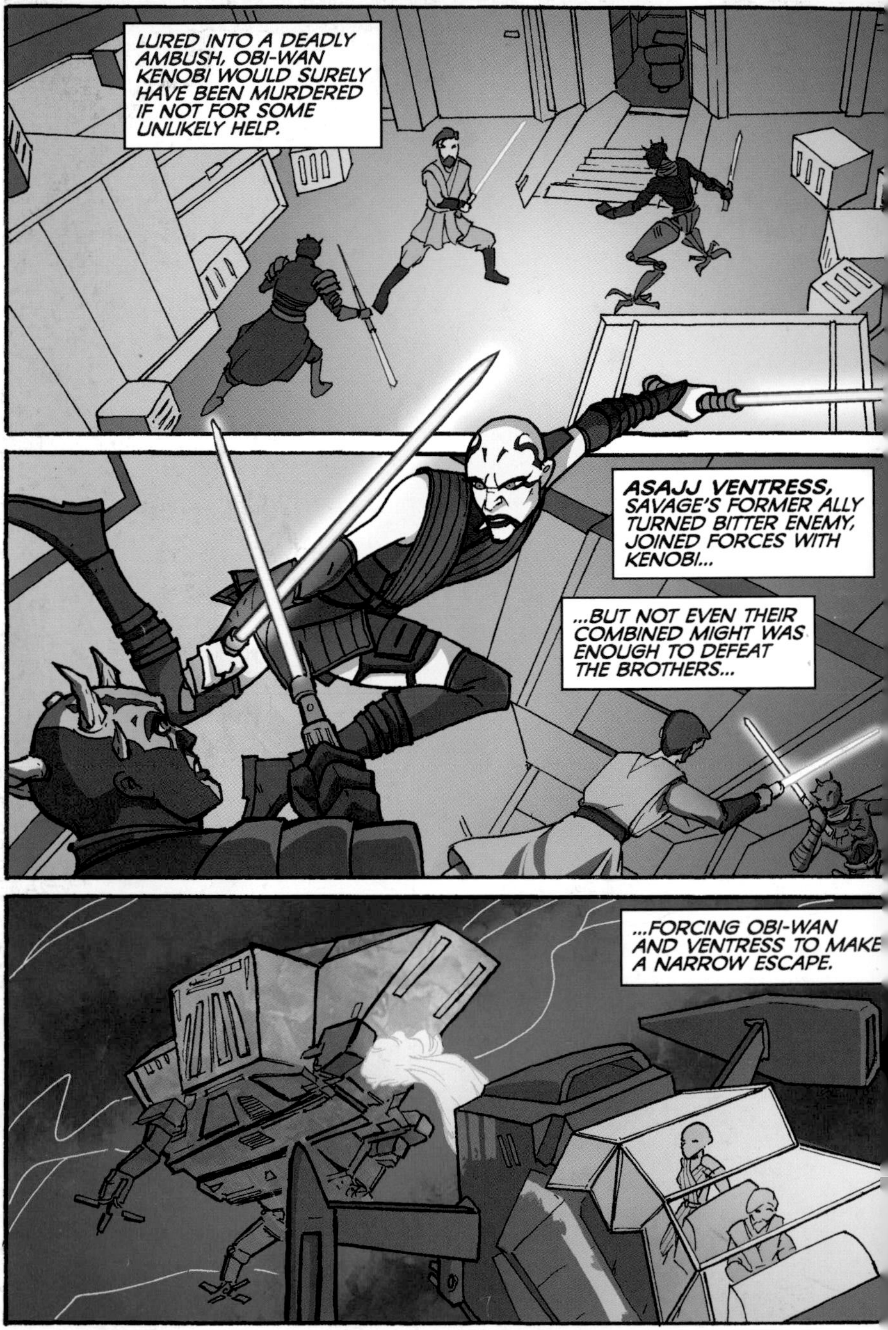
LURED INTO A DEADLY AMBUSH, OBI-WAN KENOBI WOULD SURELY HAVE BEEN MURDERED IF NOT FOR SOME UNLIKELY HELP.
ASAJJ VENTRESS, SAVAGE'S FORMER ALLY TURNED BITTER ENEMY, JOINED FORCES WITH KENOBI...
...BUT NOT EVEN THEIR COMBINED MIGHT WAS ENOUGH TO DEFEAT THE BROTHERS...
...FORCING OBI-WAN AND VENTRESS TO MAKE A NARROW ESCAPE.

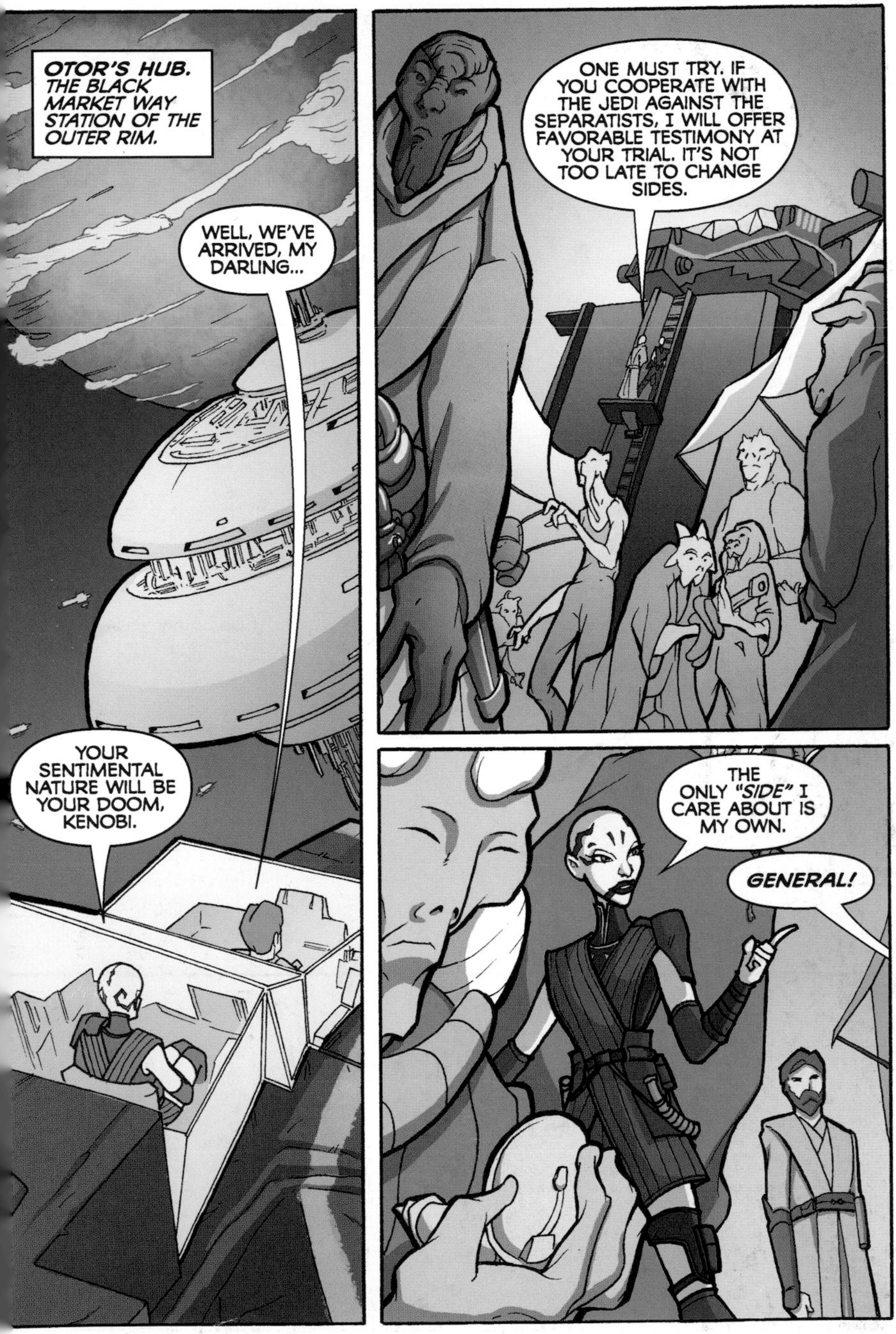
OTOR'S HUB. THE BLACK MARKET WAY STATION OF THE OUTER RIM.
WELL, WE'VE ARRIVED, MY DARLING...
YOUR SENTIMENTAL NATURE WILL BE YOUR DOOM, KENOBI.
ONE MUST TRY. IF YOU COOPERATE WITH THE JEDI AGAINST THE SEPARATISTS, I WILL OFFER FAVORABLE TESTIMONY AT YOUR TRIAL. IT'S NOT TOO LATE TO CHANGE SIDES.
THE ONLY "SIDE" I CARE ABOUT IS MY OWN.
GENERAL!

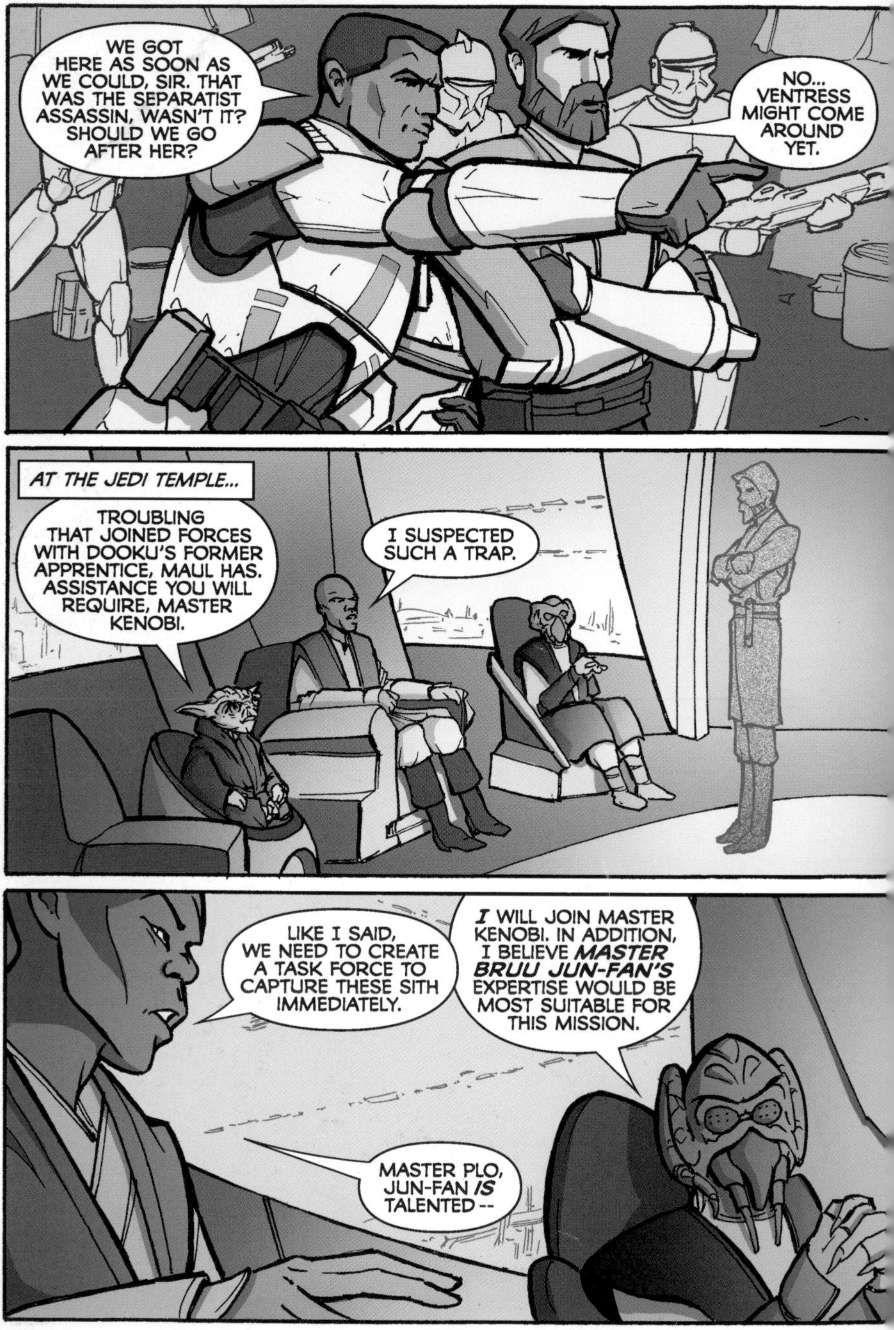
WE GOT HERE AS SOON AS WE COULD, SIR. THAT WAS THE SEPARATIST ASSASSIN, WASN'T IT? SHOULD WE GO AFTER HER?
NO... VENTRESS MIGHT COME AROUND YET.
AT THE JEDI TEMPLE...
TROUBLING THAT JOINED FORCES WITH DOOKU'S FORMER APPRENTICE, MAUL HAS. ASSISTANCE YOU WILL REQUIRE, MASTER KENOBI.
I SUSPECTED SUCH A TRAP.
LIKE I SAID, WE NEED TO CREATE A TASK FORCE TO CAPTURE THESE SITH IMMEDIATELY.
I WILL JOIN MASTER KENOBI. IN ADDITION, I BELIEVE ***MASTER BRUU JUN-FAN'S*** EXPERTISE WOULD BE MOST SUITABLE FOR THIS MISSION.
MASTER PLO, JUN-FAN *IS* TALENTED --

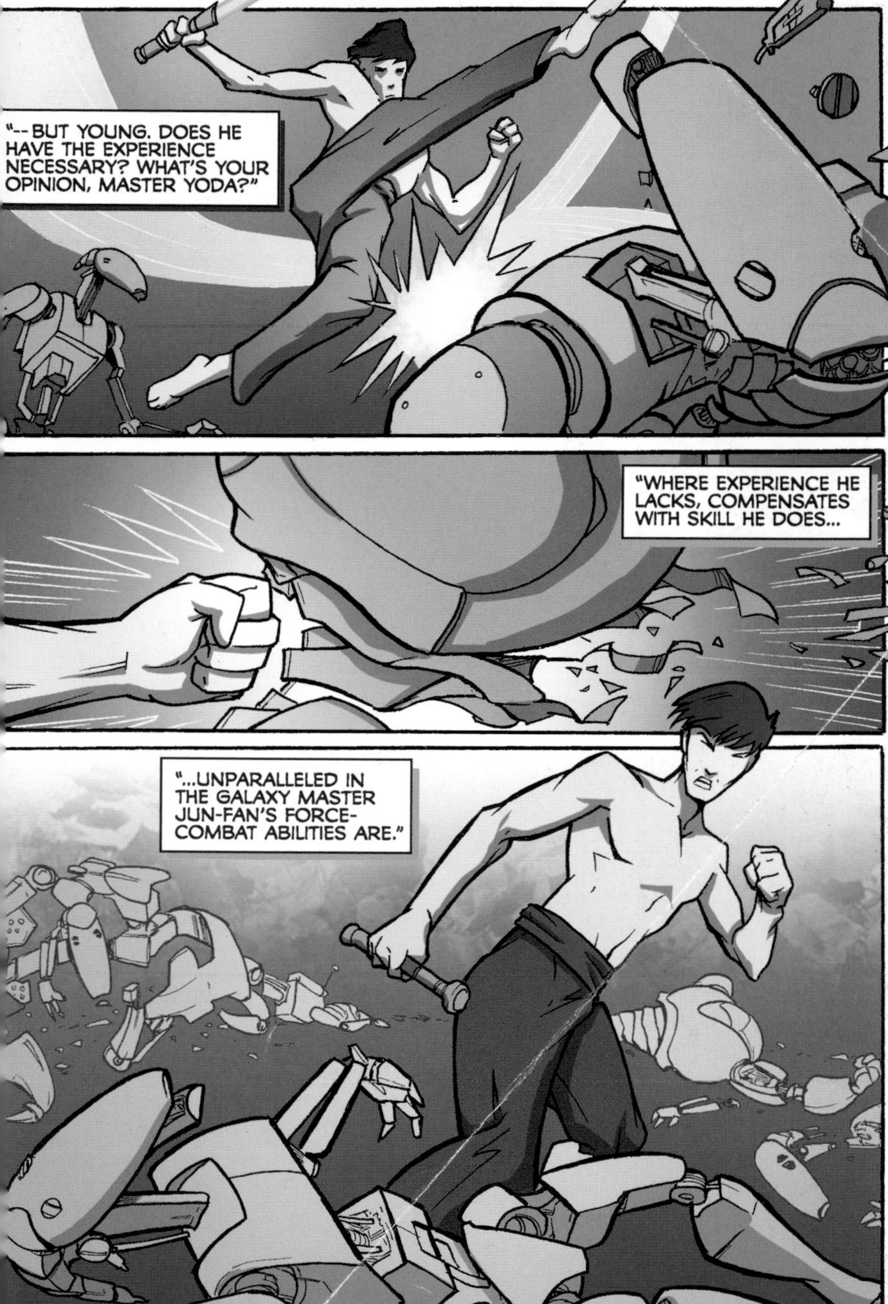
"--BUT YOUNG. DOES HE HAVE THE EXPERIENCE NECESSARY? WHAT'S YOUR OPINION, MASTER YODA?"
"WHERE EXPERIENCE HE LACKS, COMPENSATES WITH SKILL HE DOES...
"...UNPARALLELED IN THE GALAXY MASTER JUN-FAN'S FORCE-COMBAT ABILITIES ARE."

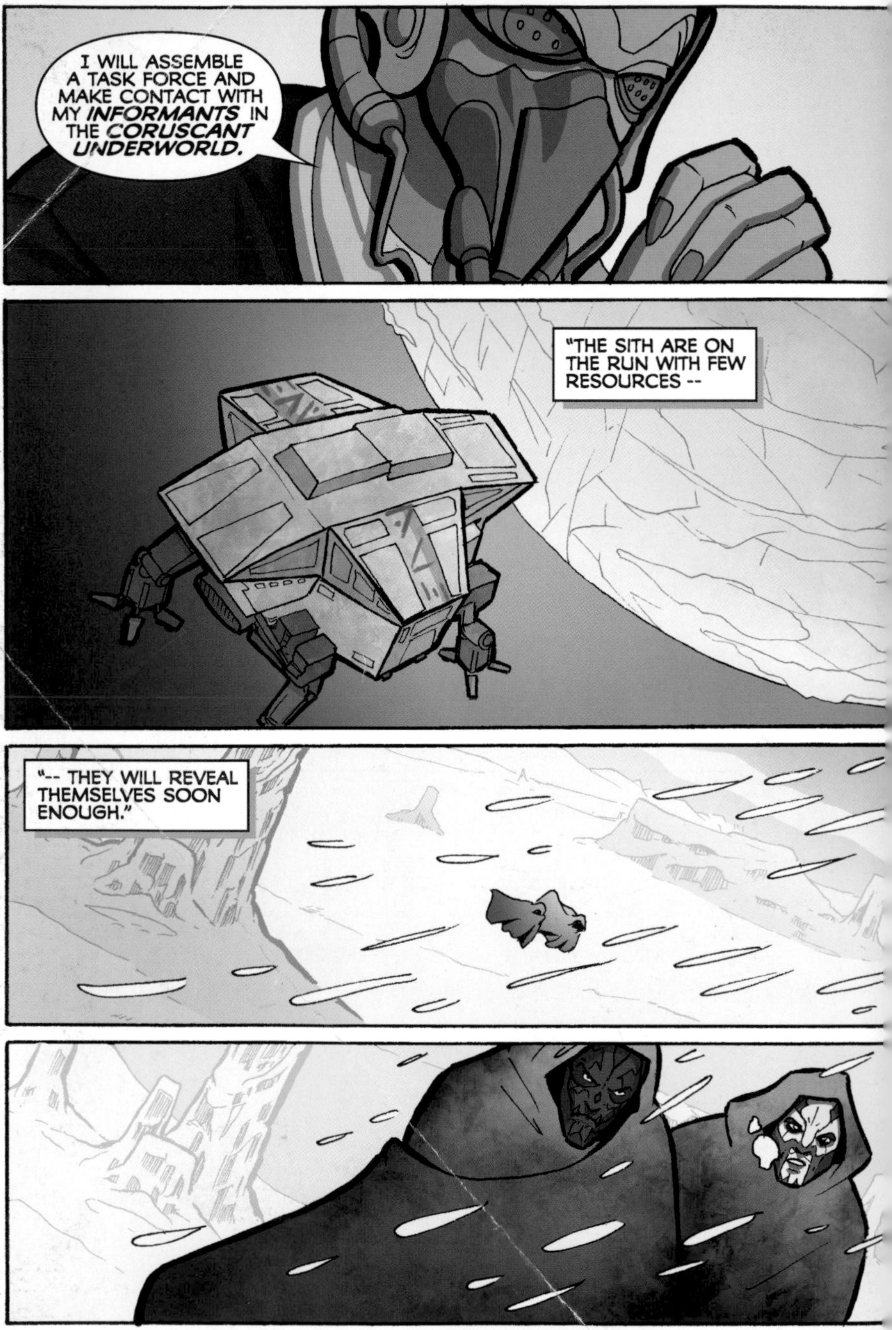
I WILL ASSEMBLE A TASK FORCE AND MAKE CONTACT WITH MY *INFORMANTS* IN THE *CORUSCANT UNDERWORLD.*
"THE SITH ARE ON THE RUN WITH FEW RESOURCES --
"-- THEY WILL REVEAL THEMSELVES SOON ENOUGH."

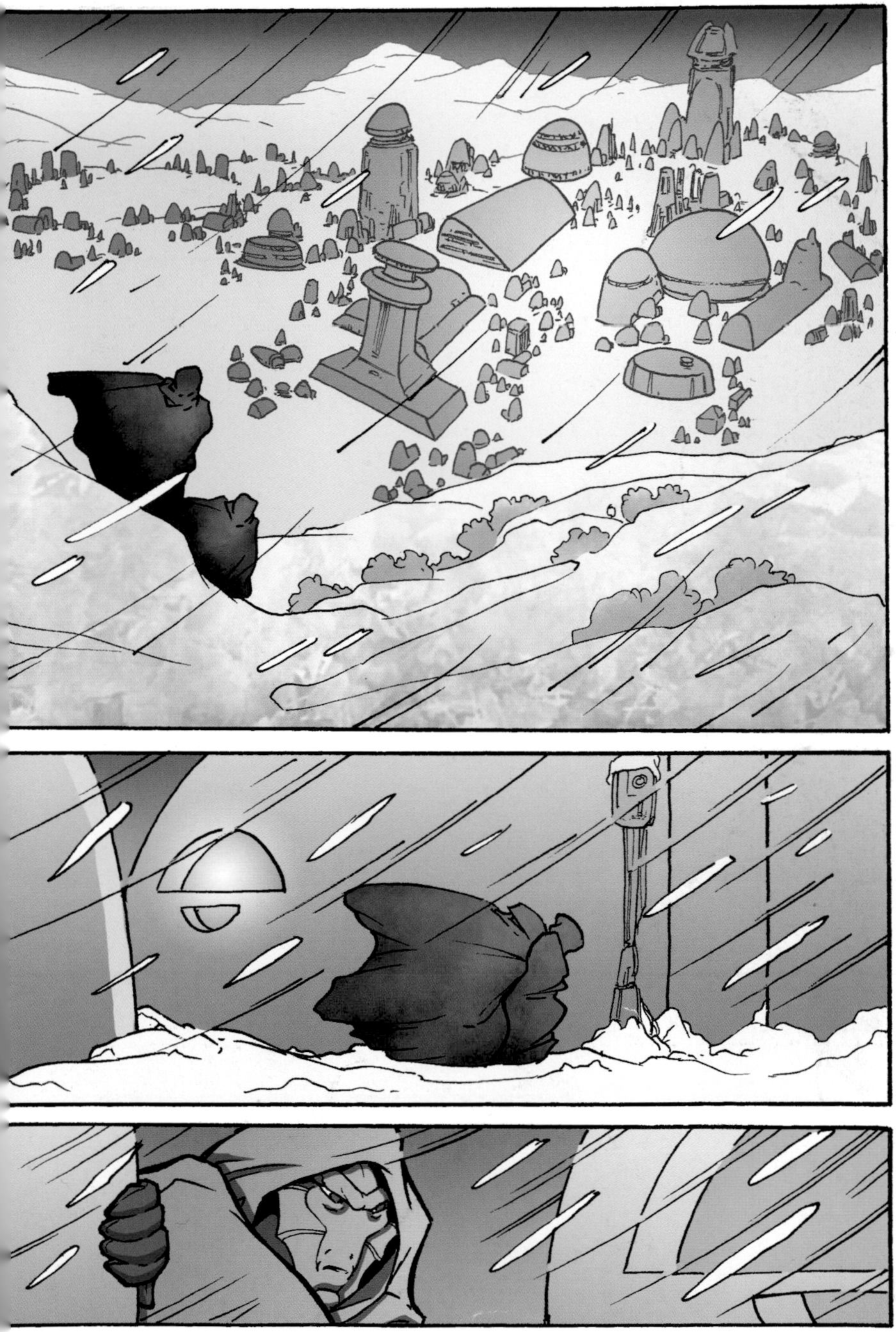

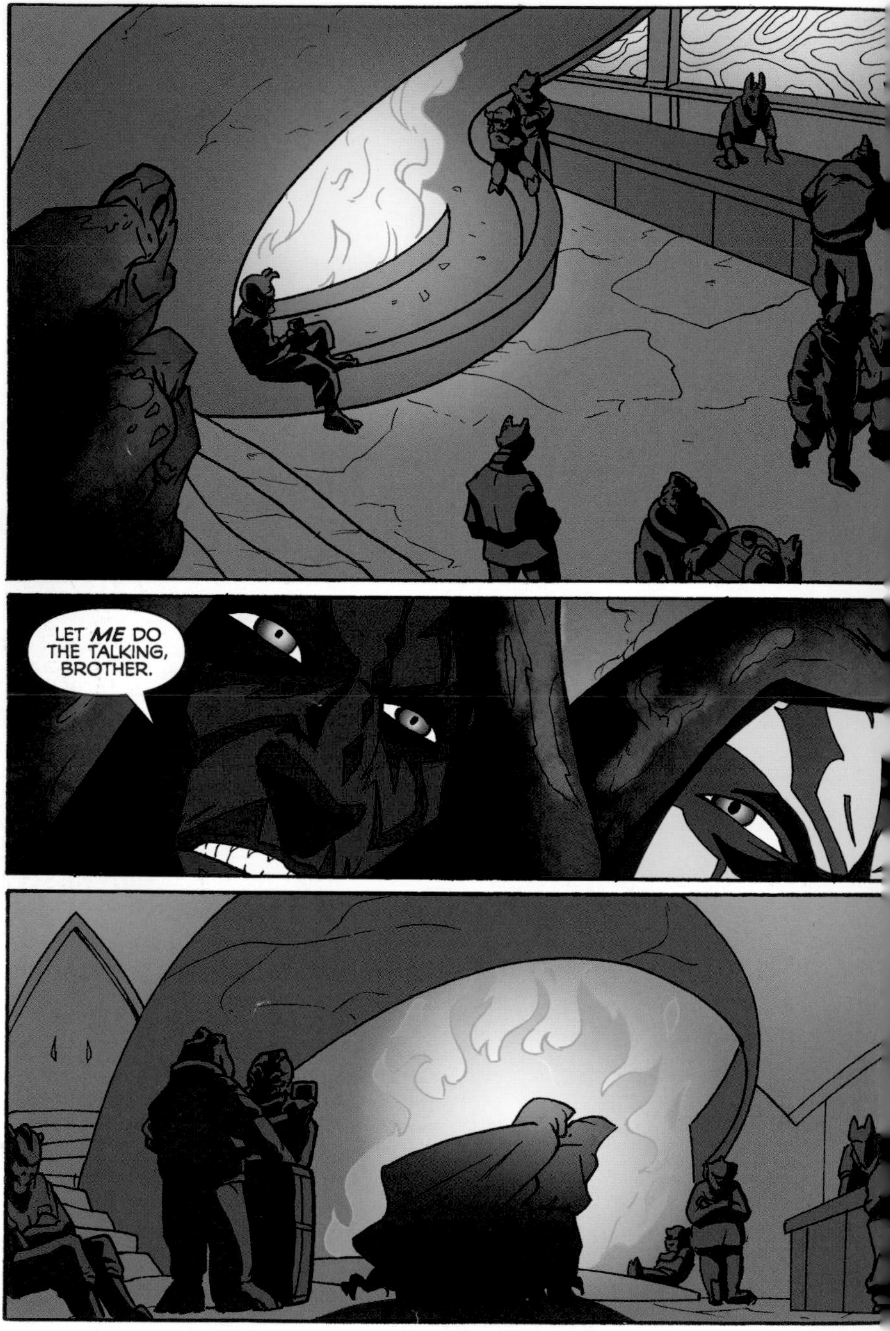
LET *ME* DO THE TALKING, BROTHER.

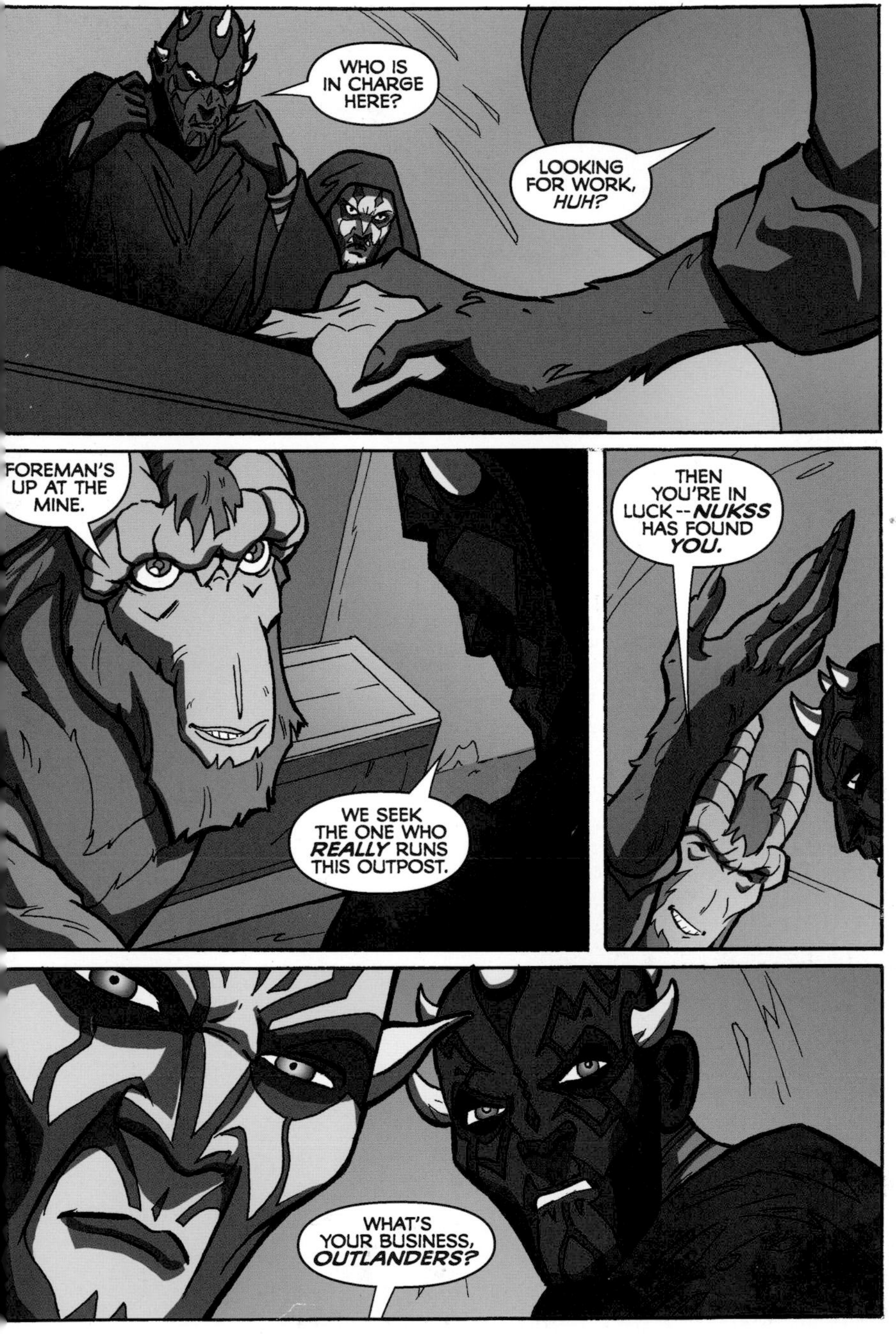
WHO IS IN CHARGE HERE?
LOOKING FOR WORK, *HUH?*
FOREMAN'S UP AT THE MINE.
WE SEEK THE ONE WHO *REALLY* RUNS THIS OUTPOST.
THEN YOU'RE IN LUCK--*NUKSS* HAS FOUND *YOU.*
WHAT'S YOUR BUSINESS, *OUTLANDERS?*

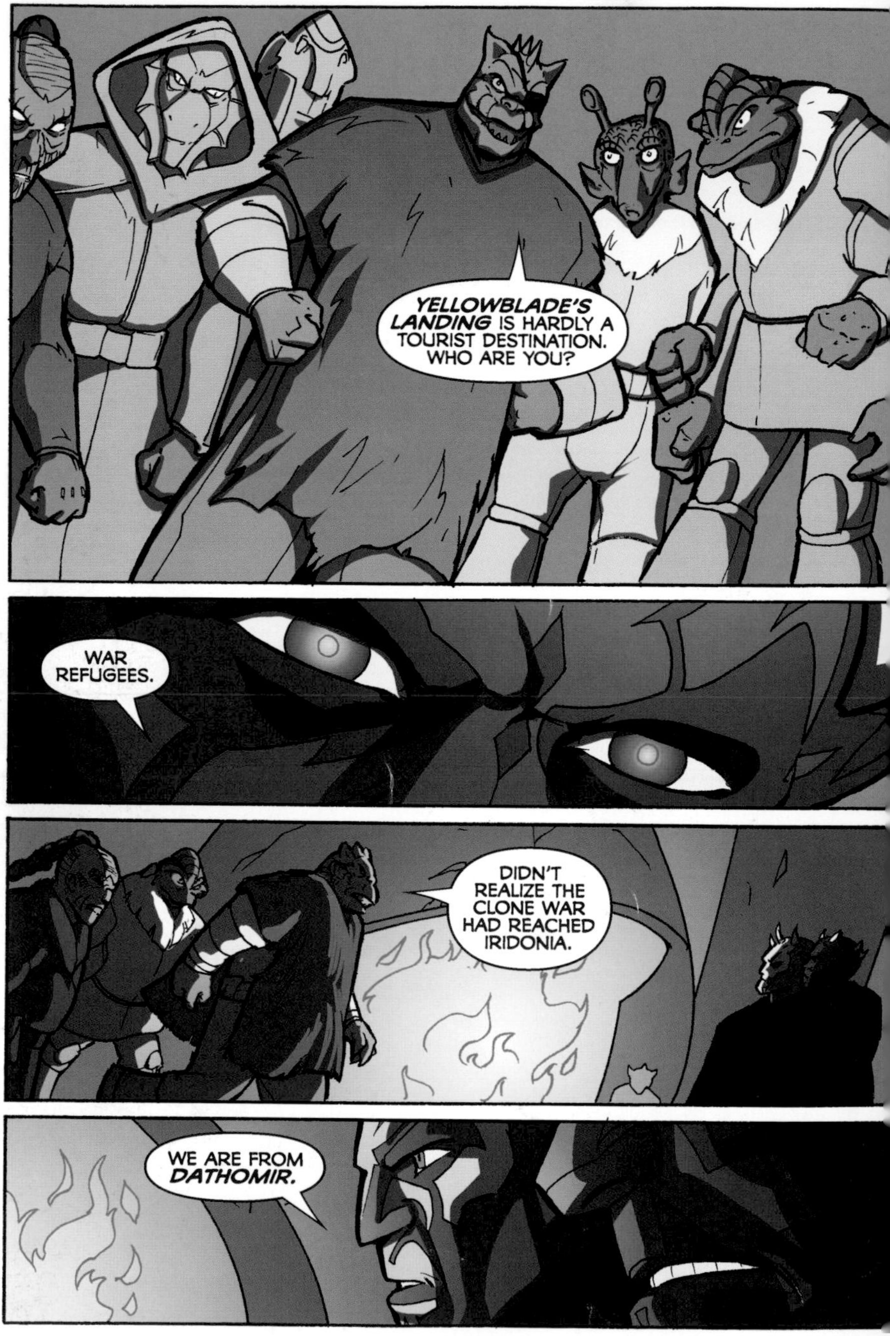
YELLOWBLADE'S LANDING IS HARDLY A TOURIST DESTINATION. WHO ARE YOU?
WAR REFUGEES.
DIDN'T REALIZE THE CLONE WAR HAD REACHED IRIDONIA.
WE ARE FROM *DATHOMIR.*

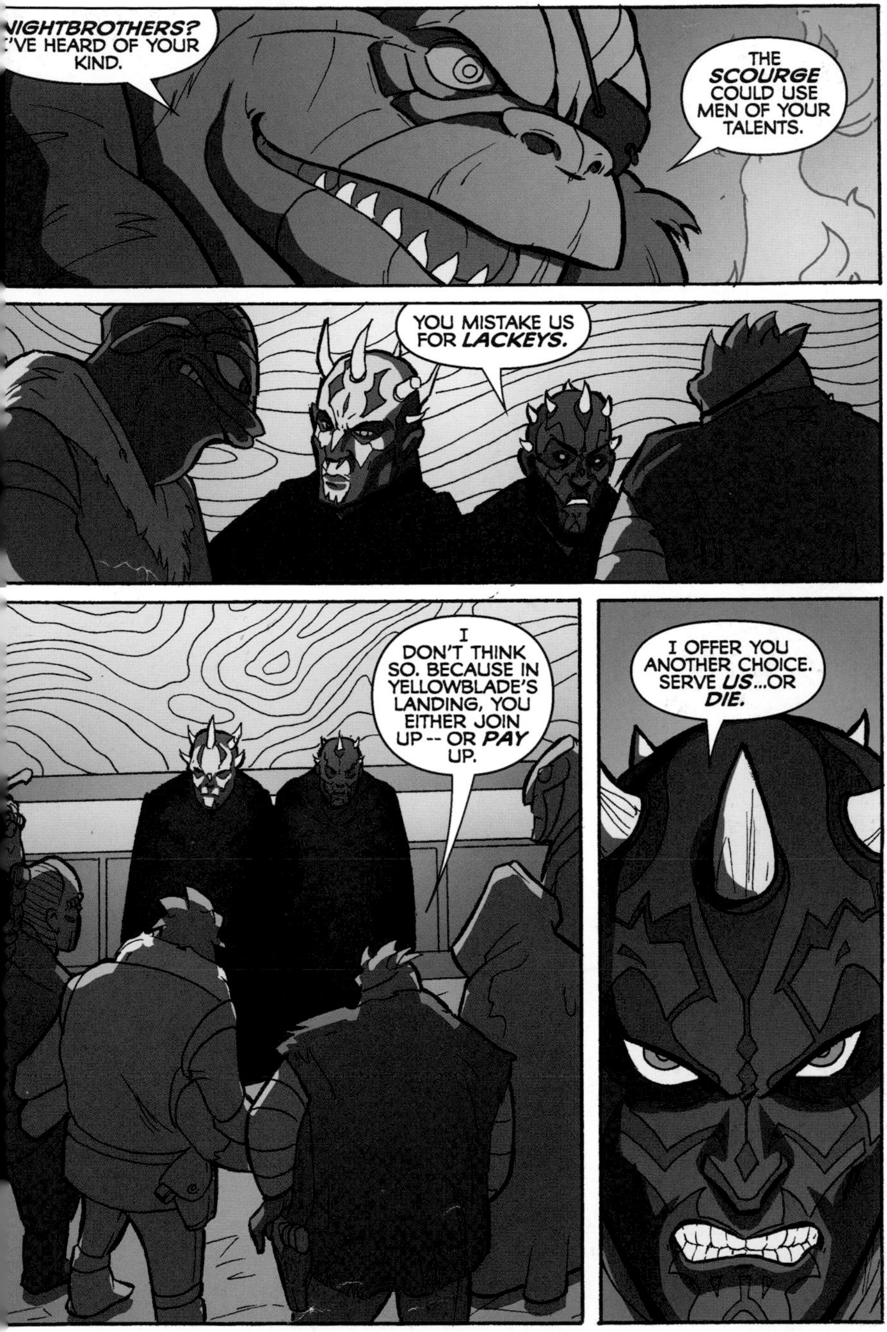

NIGHTBROTHERS? I'VE HEARD OF YOUR KIND.
THE SCOURGE COULD USE MEN OF YOUR TALENTS.
YOU MISTAKE US FOR LACKEYS.
I DON'T THINK SO. BECAUSE IN YELLOWBLADE'S LANDING, YOU EITHER JOIN UP -- OR PAY UP.
I OFFER YOU ANOTHER CHOICE. SERVE US...OR DIE.

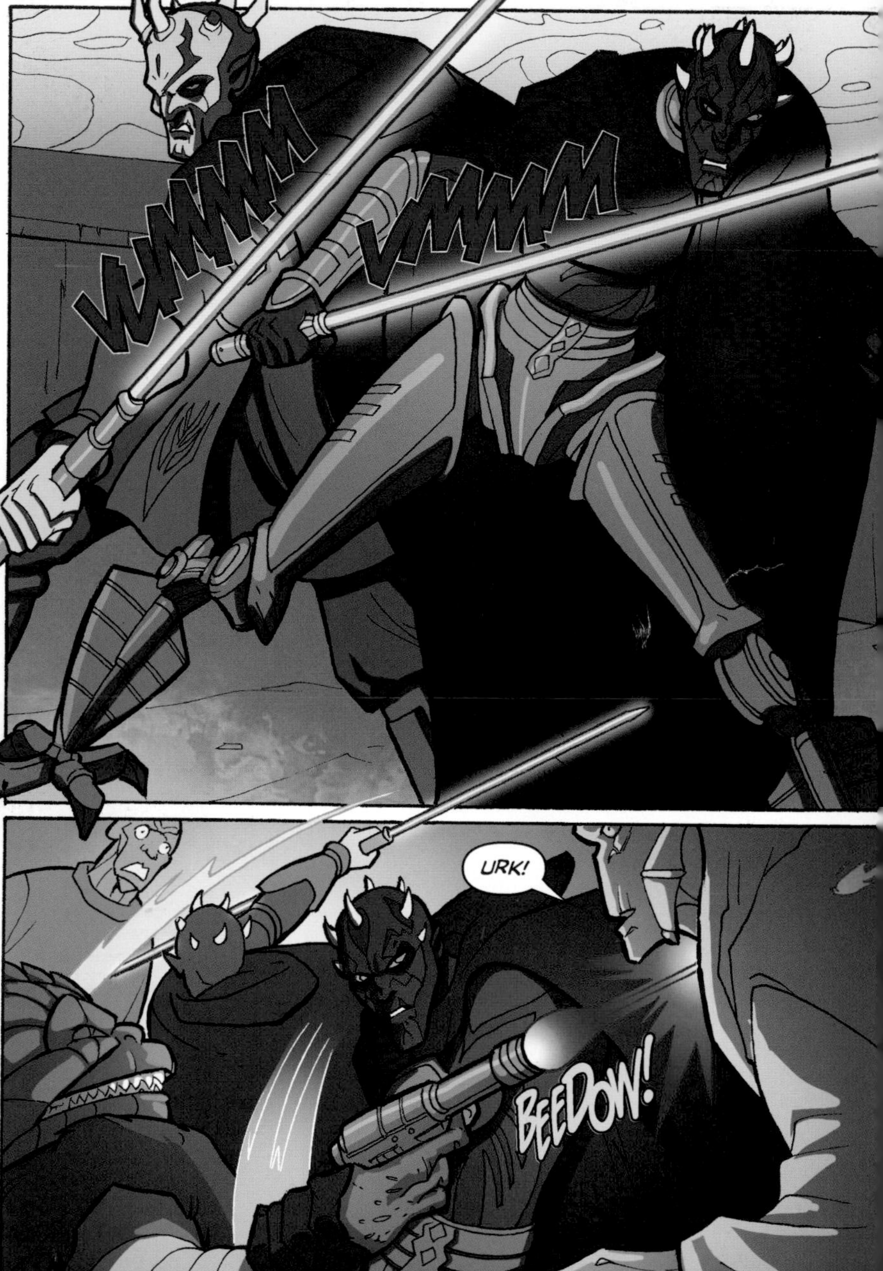
VVMMMM
VMMMMM
URK!
BEEDOW!

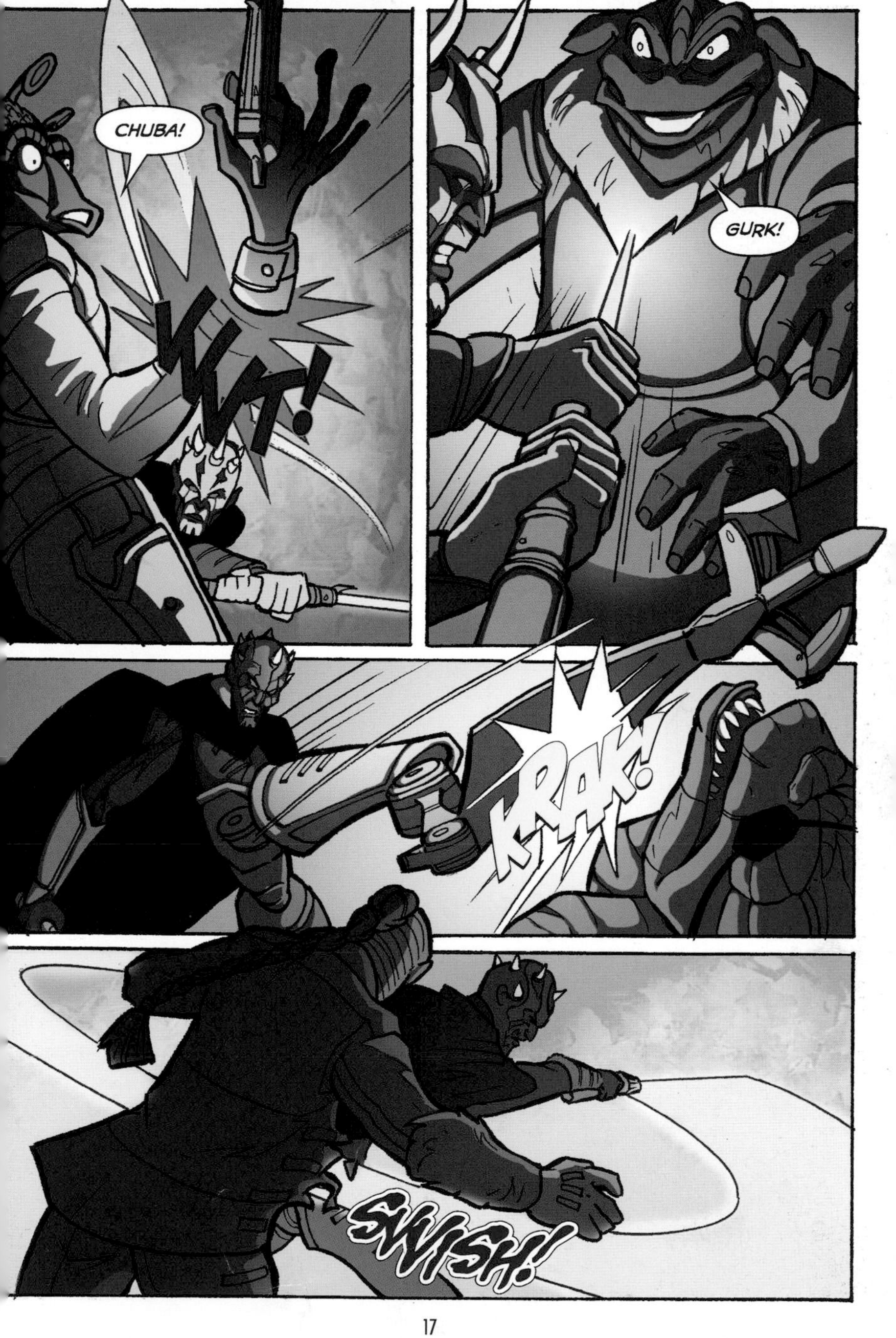
CHUBA!
WVT!
GURK!
KRAK!
SWISH!

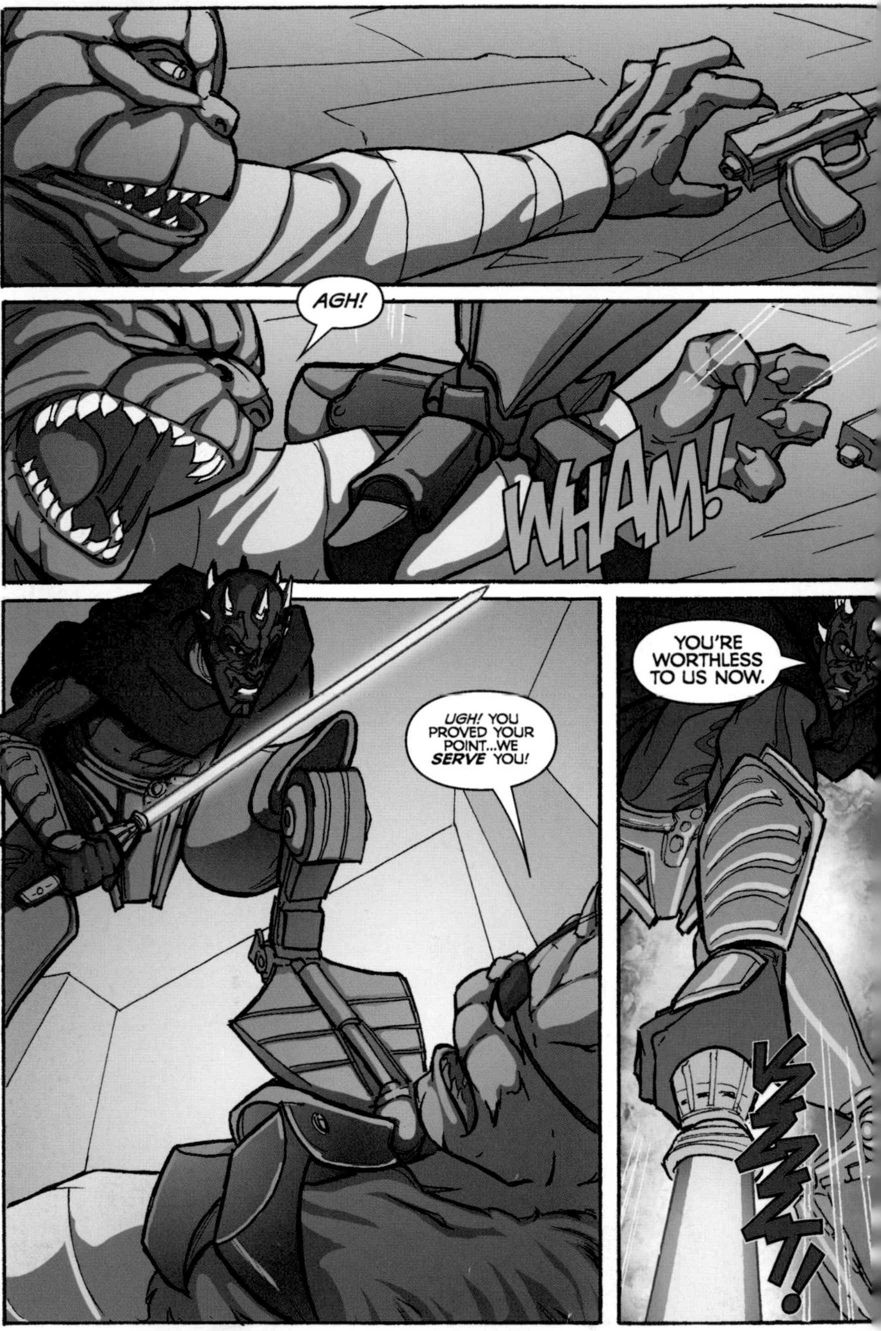
AGH!
WHAM!
UGH! YOU PROVED YOUR POINT...WE SERVE YOU!
YOU'RE WORTHLESS TO US NOW.
VVMMM!

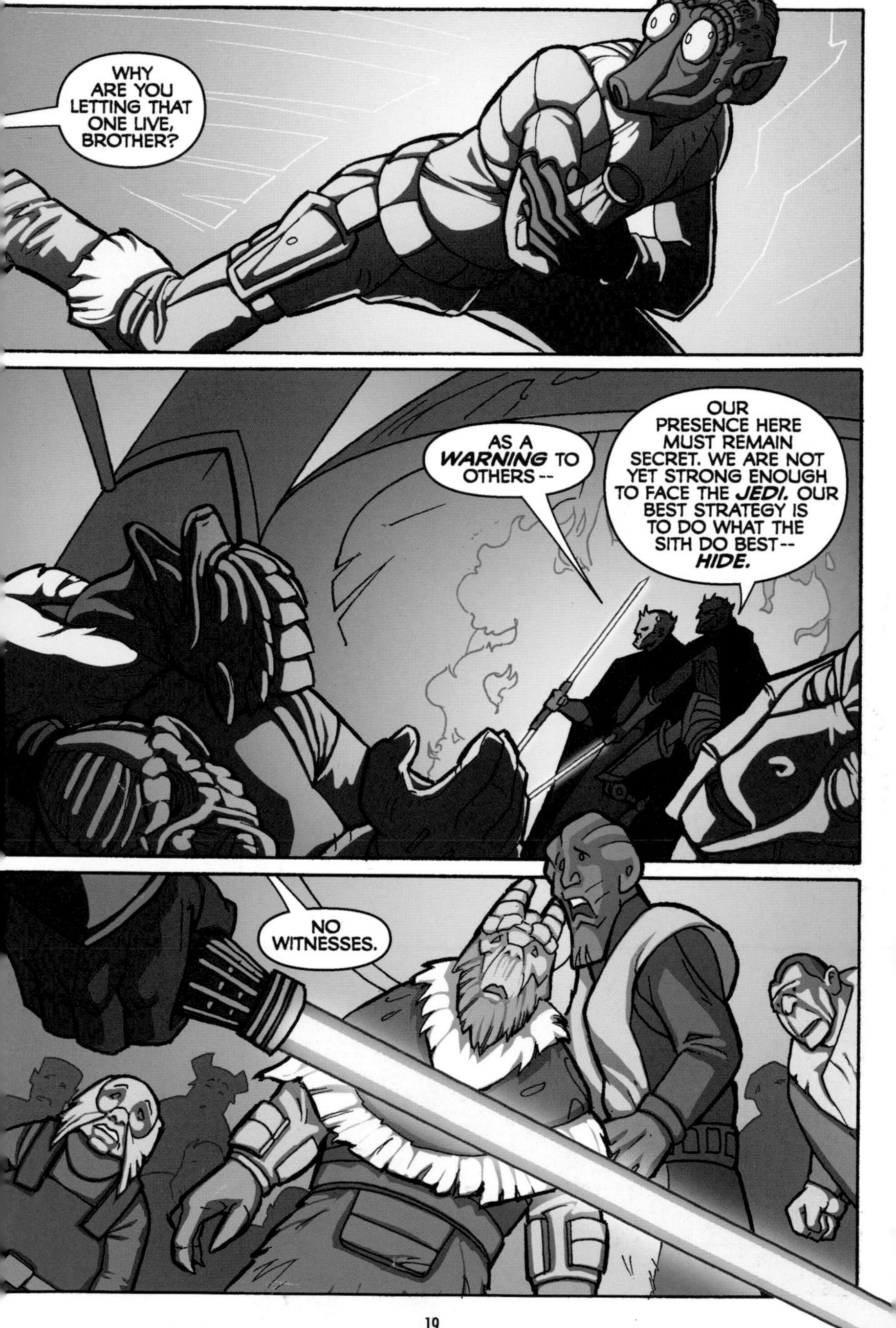
WHY ARE YOU LETTING THAT ONE LIVE, BROTHER?
AS A *WARNING* TO OTHERS--
OUR PRESENCE HERE MUST REMAIN SECRET. WE ARE NOT YET STRONG ENOUGH TO FACE THE *JEDI.* OUR BEST STRATEGY IS TO DO WHAT THE SITH DO BEST-- *HIDE.*
NO WITNESSES.

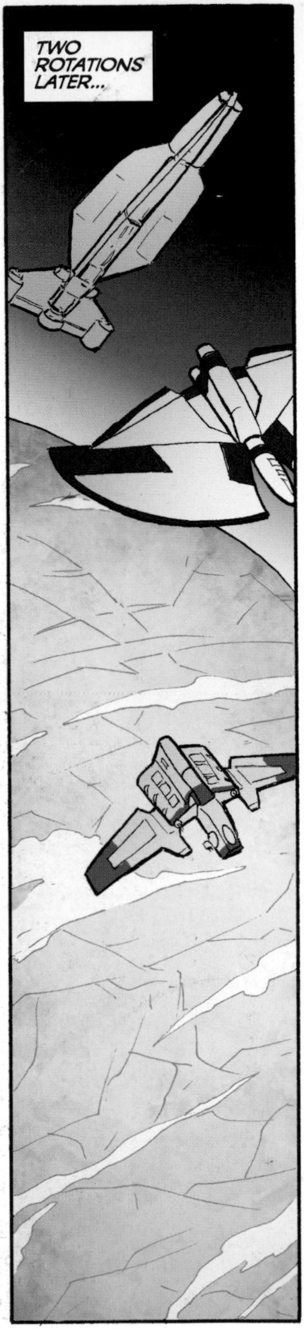
TWO ROTATIONS LATER...

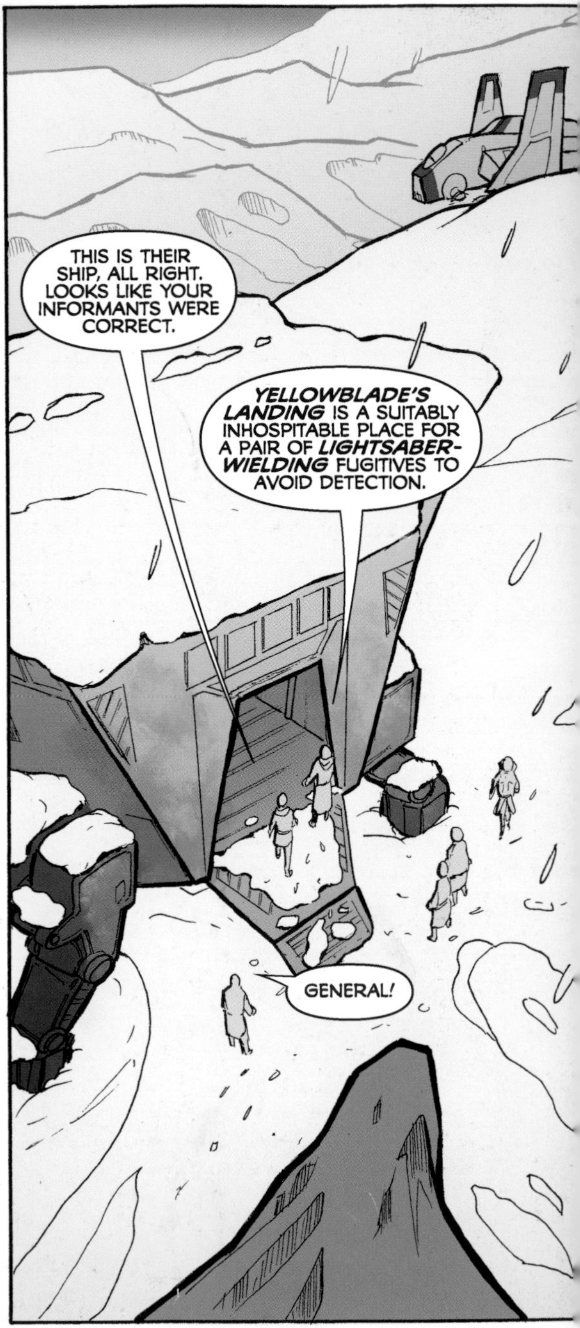
THIS IS THEIR SHIP, ALL RIGHT. LOOKS LIKE YOUR INFORMANTS WERE CORRECT.
YELLOWBLADE'S LANDING IS A SUITABLY INHOSPITABLE PLACE FOR A PAIR OF LIGHTSABER-WIELDING FUGITIVES TO AVOID DETECTION.
GENERAL!

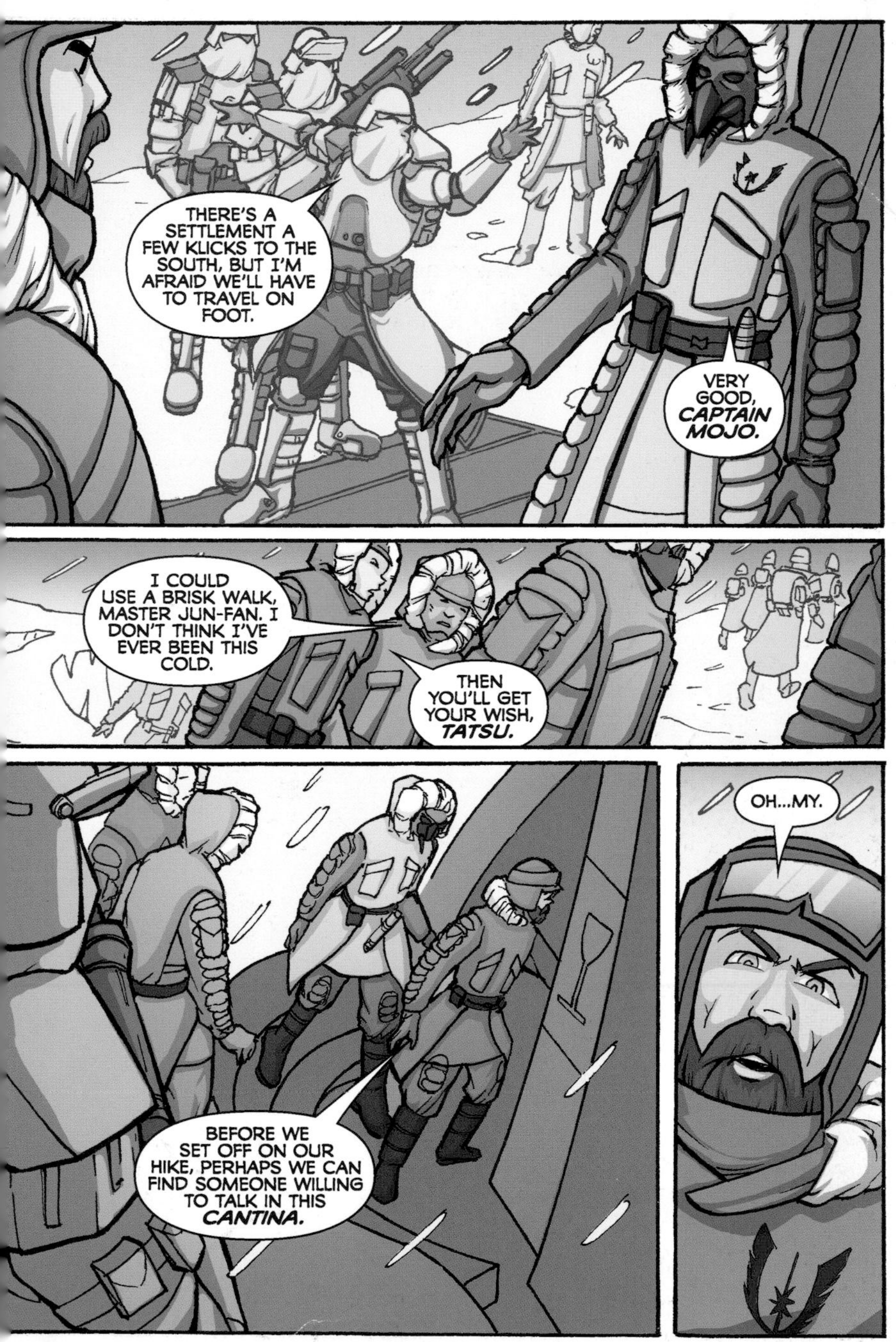
THERE'S A SETTLEMENT A FEW KLICKS TO THE SOUTH, BUT I'M AFRAID WE'LL HAVE TO TRAVEL ON FOOT.
VERY GOOD, *CAPTAIN MOJO.*
I COULD USE A BRISK WALK, MASTER JUN-FAN. I DON'T THINK I'VE EVER BEEN THIS COLD.
THEN YOU'LL GET YOUR WISH, *TATSU.*
BEFORE WE SET OFF ON OUR HIKE, PERHAPS WE CAN FIND SOMEONE WILLING TO TALK IN THIS *CANTINA.*
OH...MY.

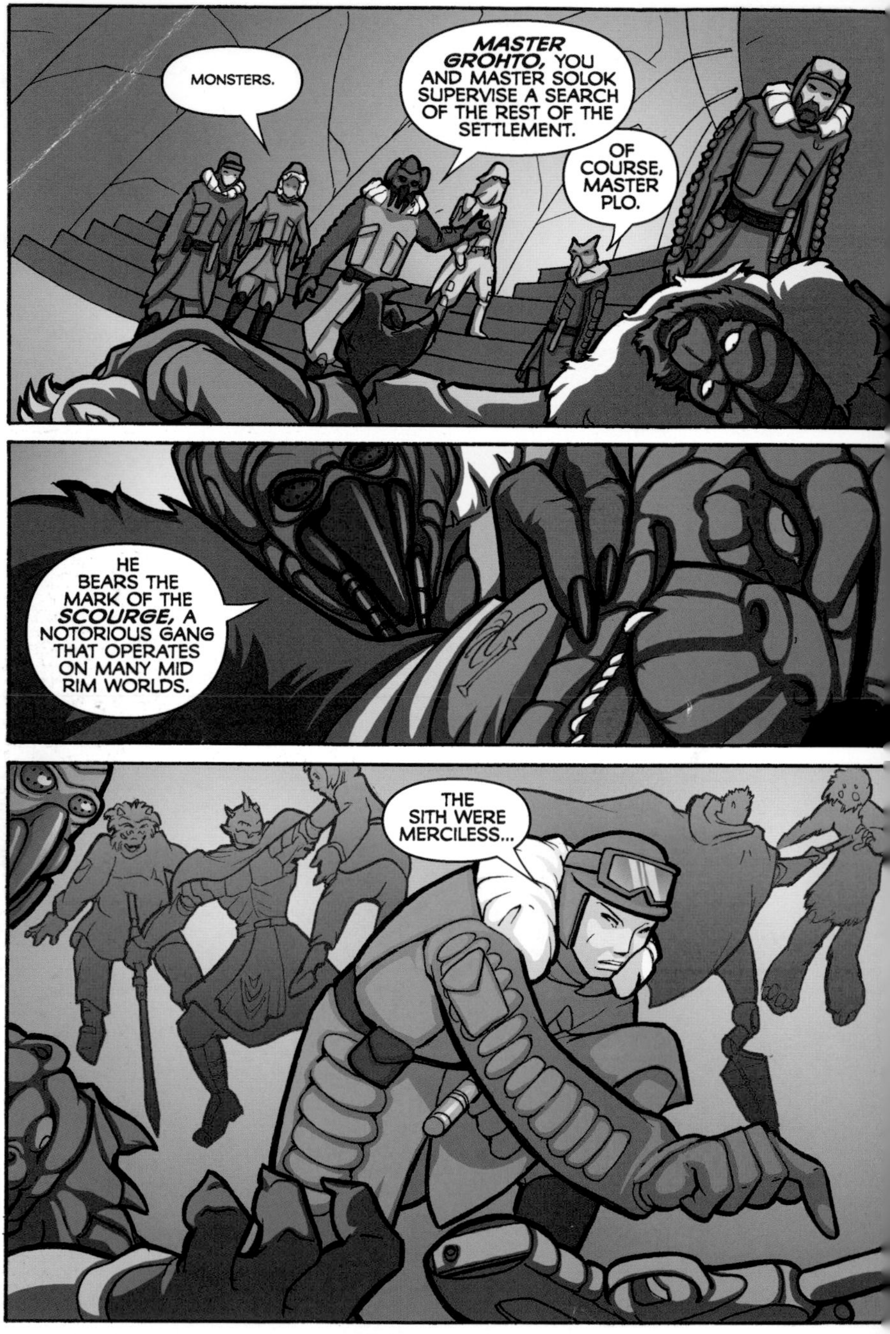
MONSTERS.
MASTER GROHTO, YOU AND MASTER SOLOK SUPERVISE A SEARCH OF THE REST OF THE SETTLEMENT.
OF COURSE, MASTER PLO.
HE BEARS THE MARK OF THE SCOURGE, A NOTORIOUS GANG THAT OPERATES ON MANY MID RIM WORLDS.
THE SITH WERE MERCILESS...

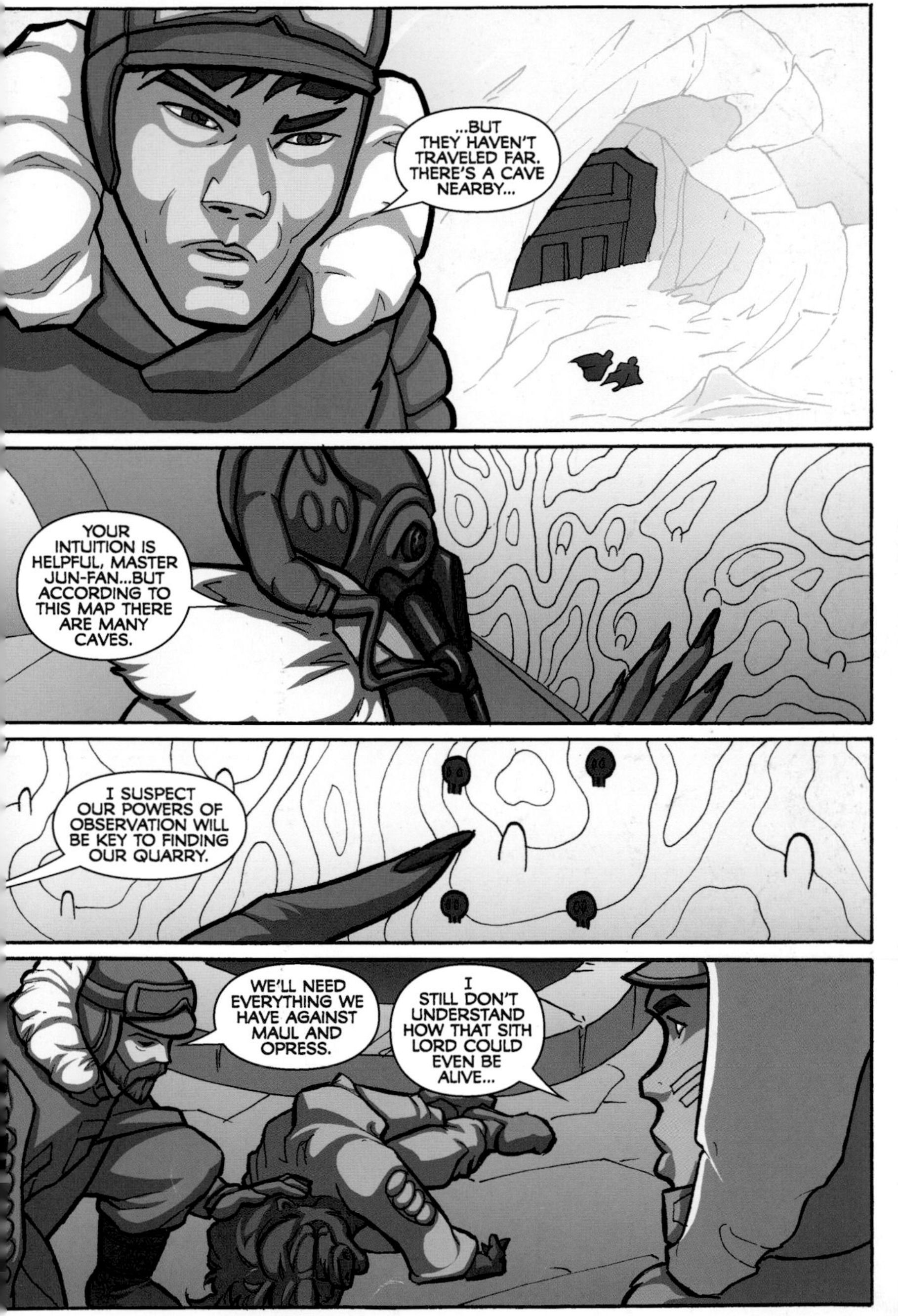
...BUT THEY HAVEN'T TRAVELED FAR. THERE'S A CAVE NEARBY...
YOUR INTUITION IS HELPFUL, MASTER JUN-FAN...BUT ACCORDING TO THIS MAP THERE ARE MANY CAVES.
I SUSPECT OUR POWERS OF OBSERVATION WILL BE KEY TO FINDING OUR QUARRY.
WE'LL NEED EVERYTHING WE HAVE AGAINST MAUL AND OPRESS.
I STILL DON'T UNDERSTAND HOW THAT SITH LORD COULD EVEN BE ALIVE...

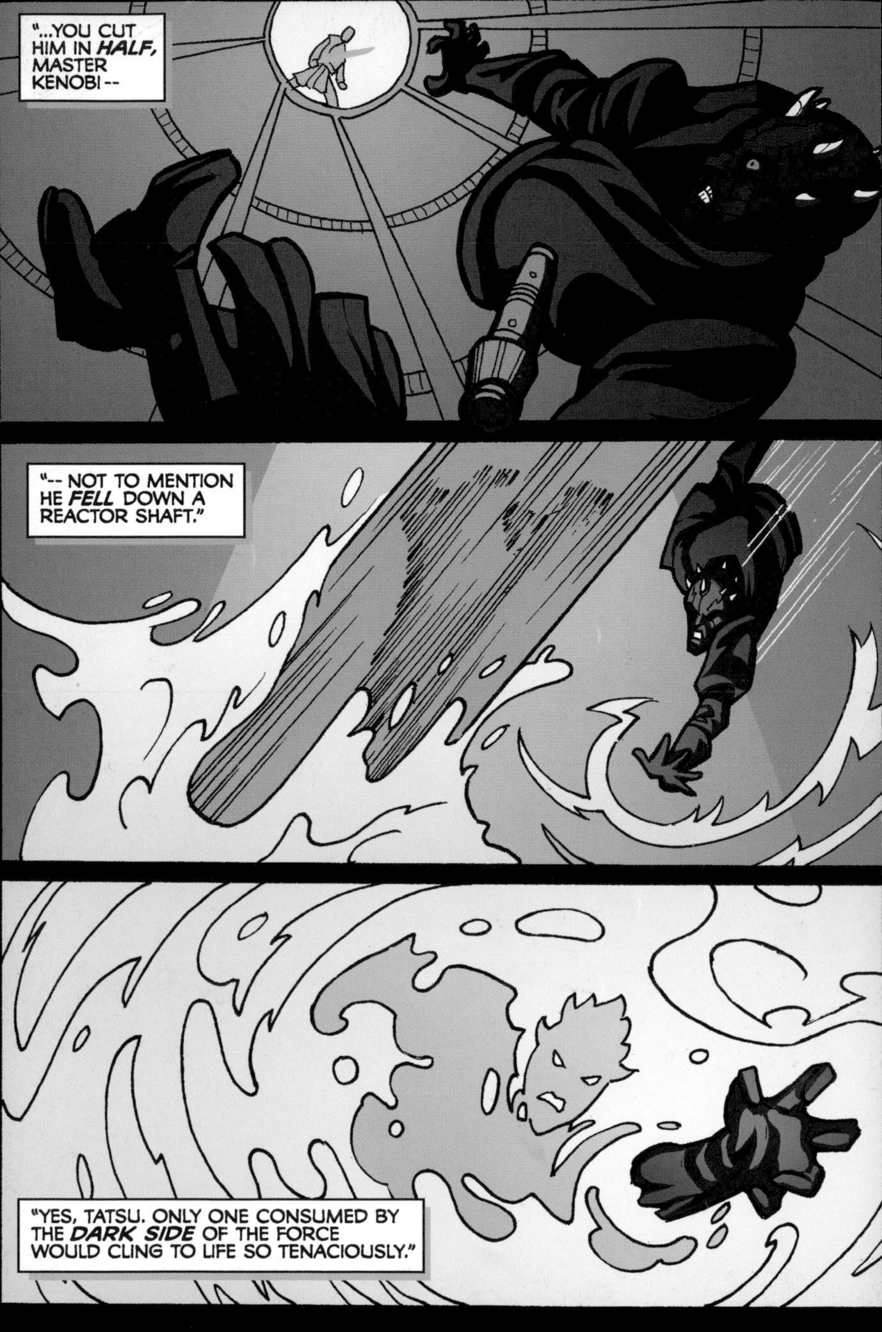
"...YOU CUT HIM IN HALF, MASTER KENOBI --
"-- NOT TO MENTION HE FELL DOWN A REACTOR SHAFT."
"YES, TATSU. ONLY ONE CONSUMED BY THE DARK SIDE OF THE FORCE WOULD CLING TO LIFE SO TENACIOUSLY."

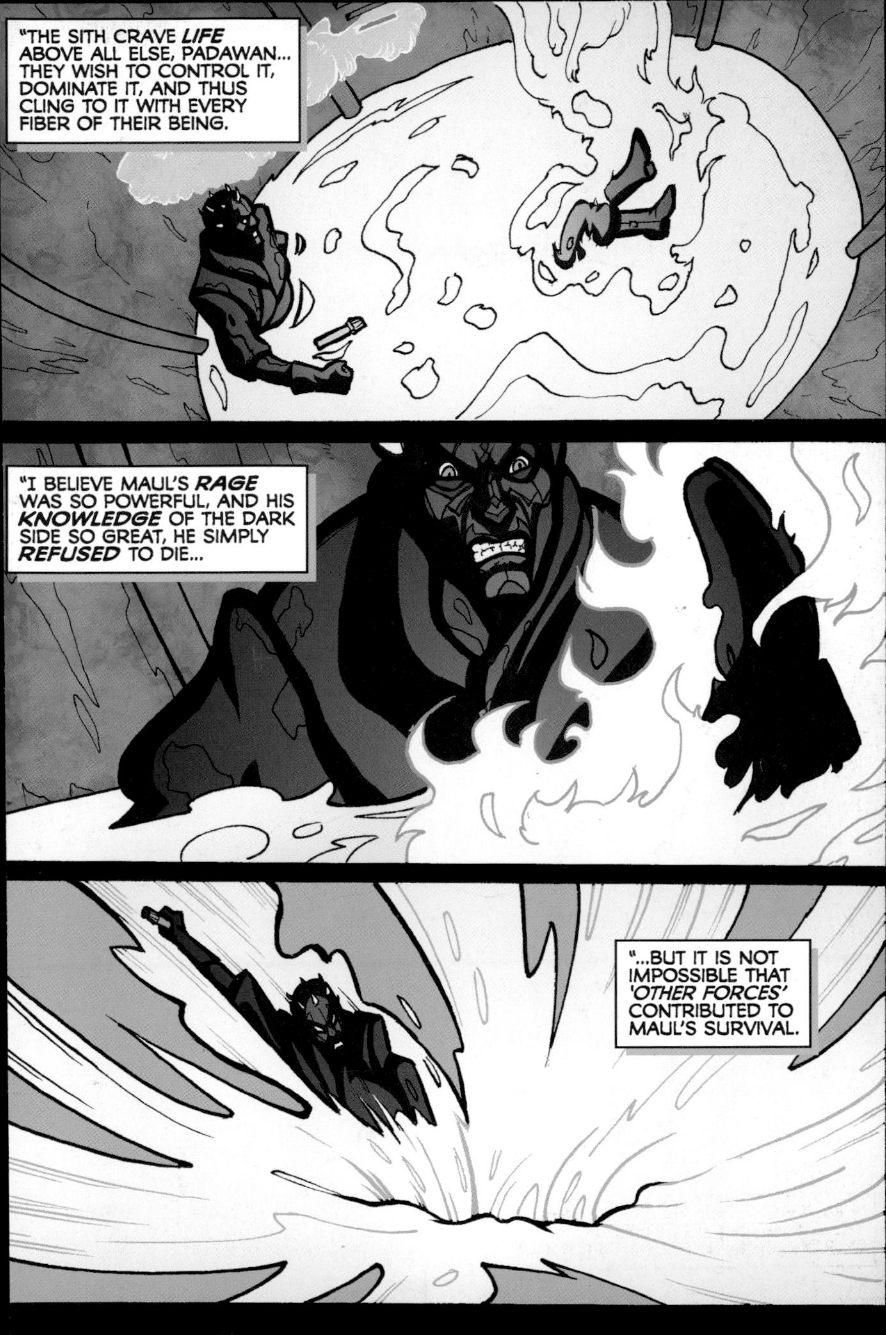
"THE SITH CRAVE *LIFE* ABOVE ALL ELSE, PADAWAN... THEY WISH TO CONTROL IT, DOMINATE IT, AND THUS CLING TO IT WITH EVERY FIBER OF THEIR BEING.
"I BELIEVE MAUL'S ***RAGE*** WAS SO POWERFUL, AND HIS ***KNOWLEDGE*** OF THE DARK SIDE SO GREAT, HE SIMPLY ***REFUSED*** TO DIE...
"...BUT IT IS NOT IMPOSSIBLE THAT *'OTHER FORCES'* CONTRIBUTED TO MAUL'S SURVIVAL.

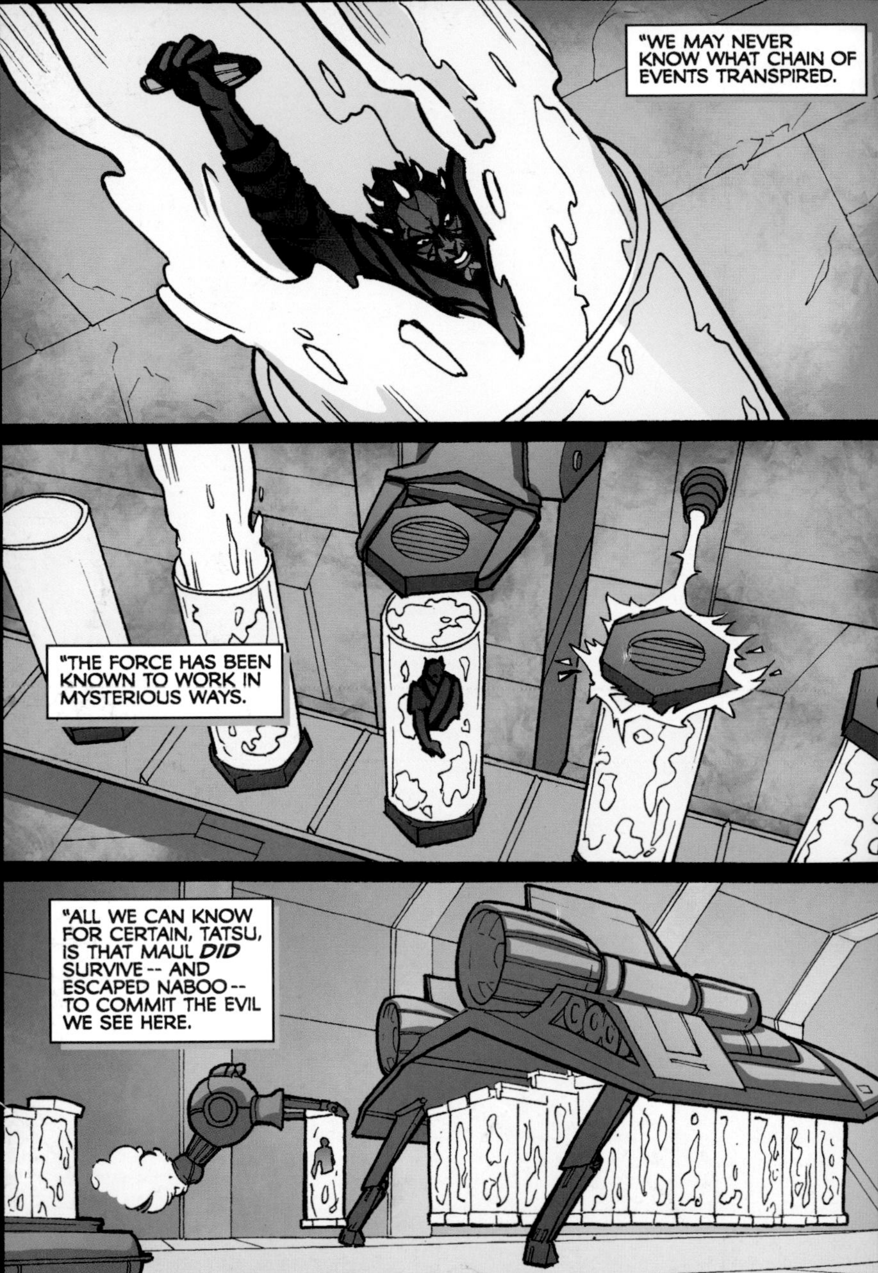
"WE MAY NEVER KNOW WHAT CHAIN OF EVENTS TRANSPIRED.
"THE FORCE HAS BEEN KNOWN TO WORK IN MYSTERIOUS WAYS.
"ALL WE CAN KNOW FOR CERTAIN, TATSU, IS THAT MAUL *DID* SURVIVE -- AND ESCAPED NABOO -- TO COMMIT THE EVIL WE SEE HERE.

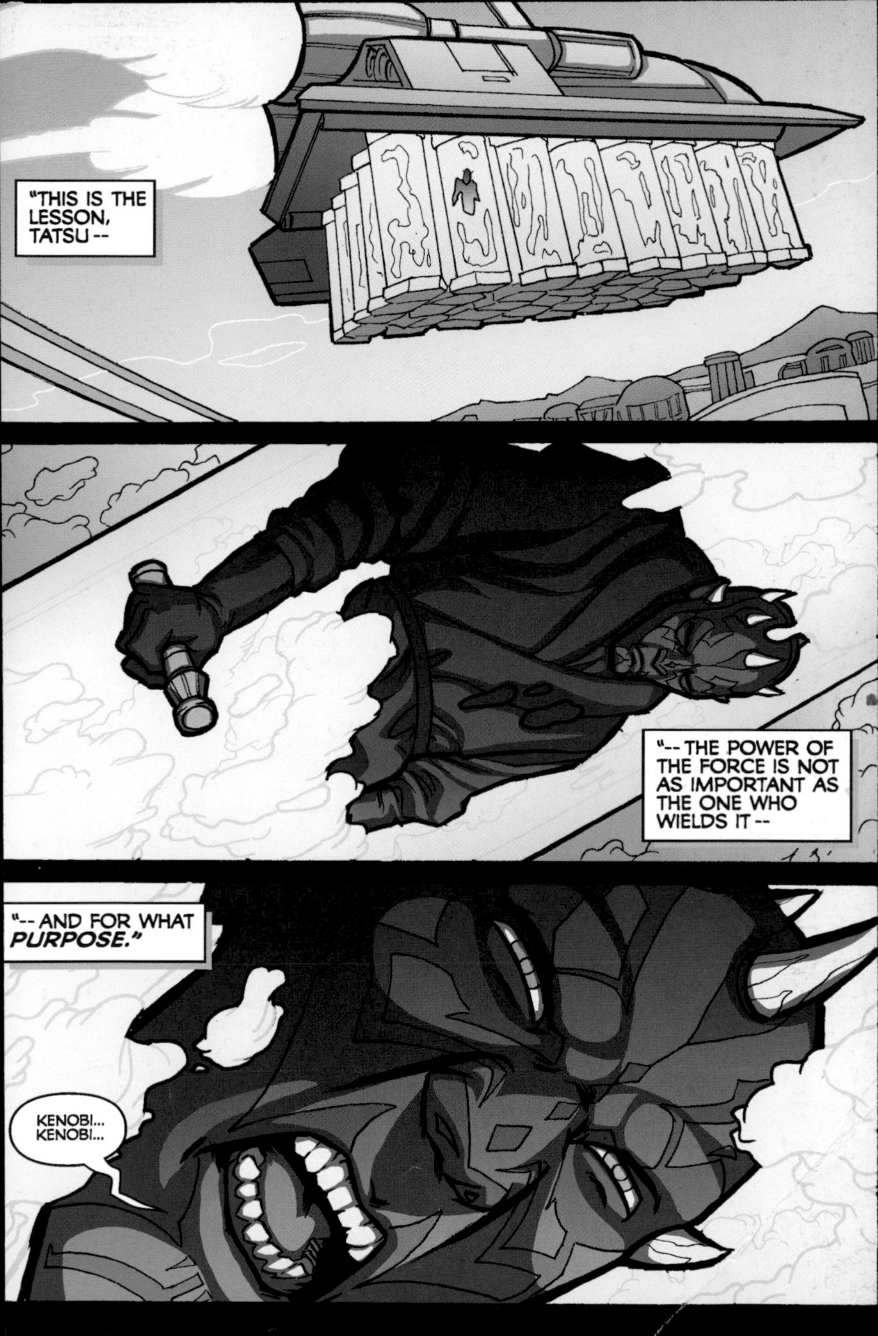
"THIS IS THE LESSON, TATSU --
"-- THE POWER OF THE FORCE IS NOT AS IMPORTANT AS THE ONE WHO WIELDS IT --
"-- AND FOR WHAT *PURPOSE.*"
KENOBI... KENOBI...

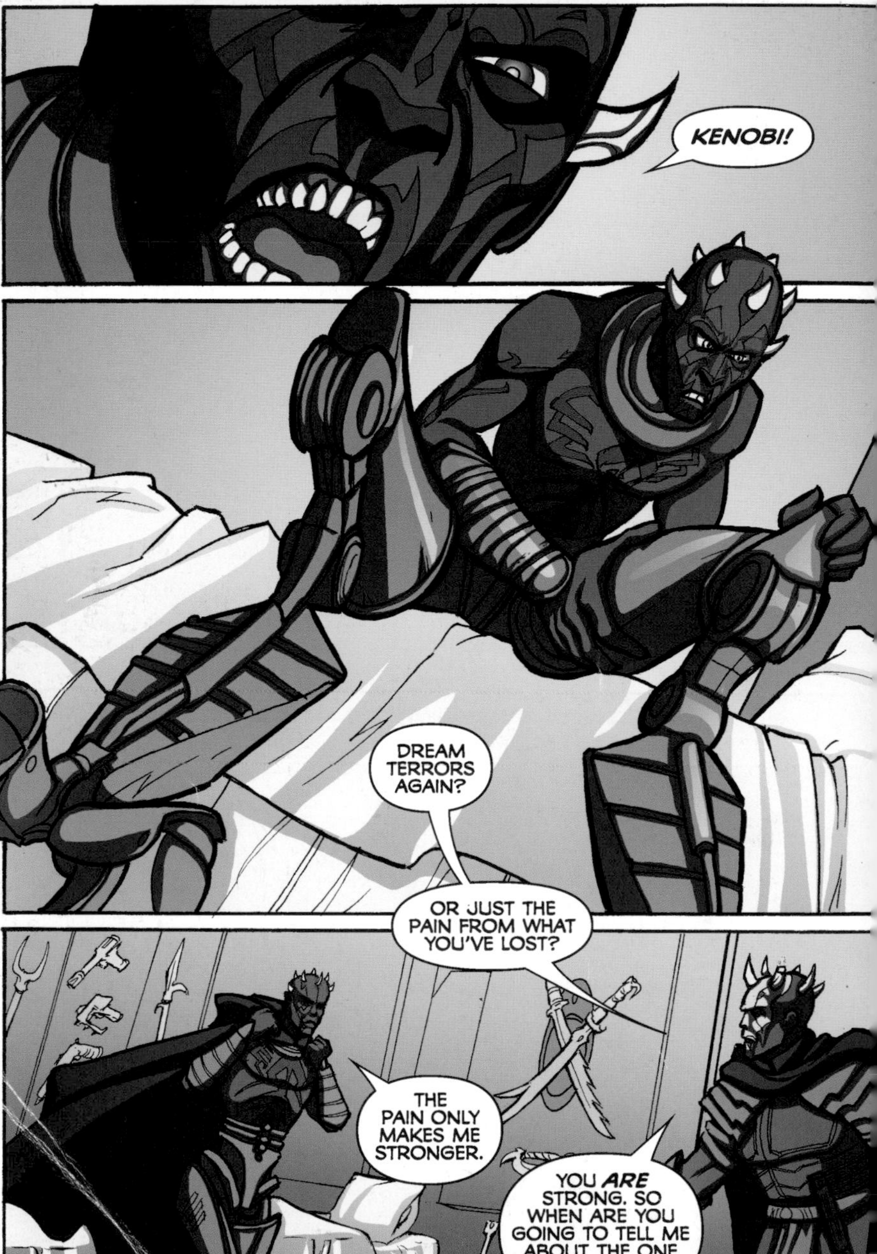
KENOBI!
DREAM TERRORS AGAIN?
OR JUST THE PAIN FROM WHAT YOU'VE LOST?
THE PAIN ONLY MAKES ME STRONGER.
YOU *ARE* STRONG. SO WHEN ARE YOU GOING TO TELL ME ABOUT THE ONE WHO TRAINED YOU?

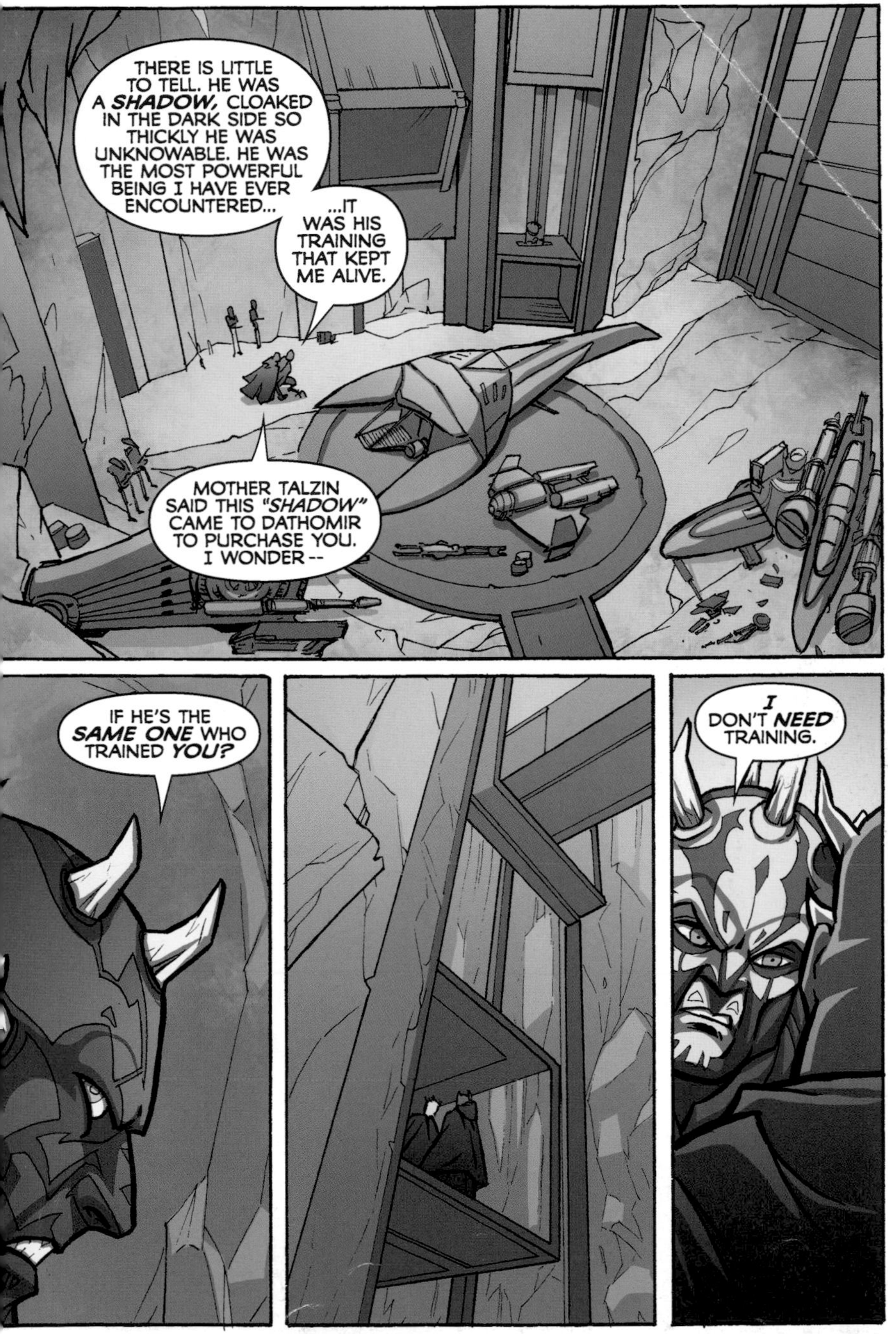
THERE IS LITTLE TO TELL. HE WAS A SHADOW, CLOAKED IN THE DARK SIDE SO THICKLY HE WAS UNKNOWABLE. HE WAS THE MOST POWERFUL BEING I HAVE EVER ENCOUNTERED...
...IT WAS HIS TRAINING THAT KEPT ME ALIVE.
MOTHER TALZIN SAID THIS "SHADOW" CAME TO DATHOMIR TO PURCHASE YOU. I WONDER --
IF HE'S THE SAME ONE WHO TRAINED YOU?
I DON'T NEED TRAINING.

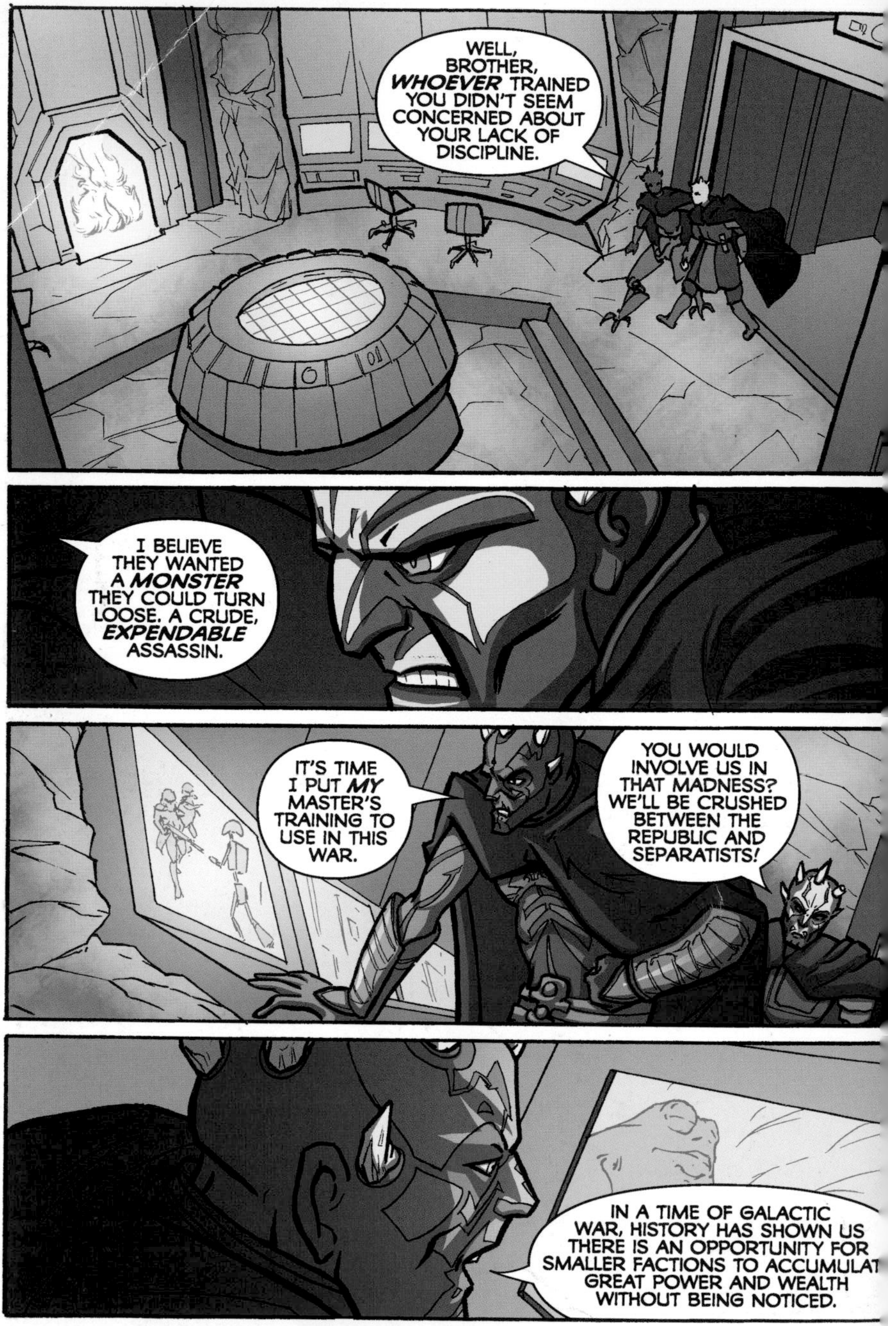
WELL, BROTHER, WHOEVER TRAINED YOU DIDN'T SEEM CONCERNED ABOUT YOUR LACK OF DISCIPLINE.
I BELIEVE THEY WANTED A MONSTER THEY COULD TURN LOOSE. A CRUDE, EXPENDABLE ASSASSIN.
IT'S TIME I PUT MY MASTER'S TRAINING TO USE IN THIS WAR.
YOU WOULD INVOLVE US IN THAT MADNESS? WE'LL BE CRUSHED BETWEEN THE REPUBLIC AND SEPARATISTS!
IN A TIME OF GALACTIC WAR, HISTORY HAS SHOWN US THERE IS AN OPPORTUNITY FOR SMALLER FACTIONS TO ACCUMULAT GREAT POWER AND WEALTH WITHOUT BEING NOTICED.

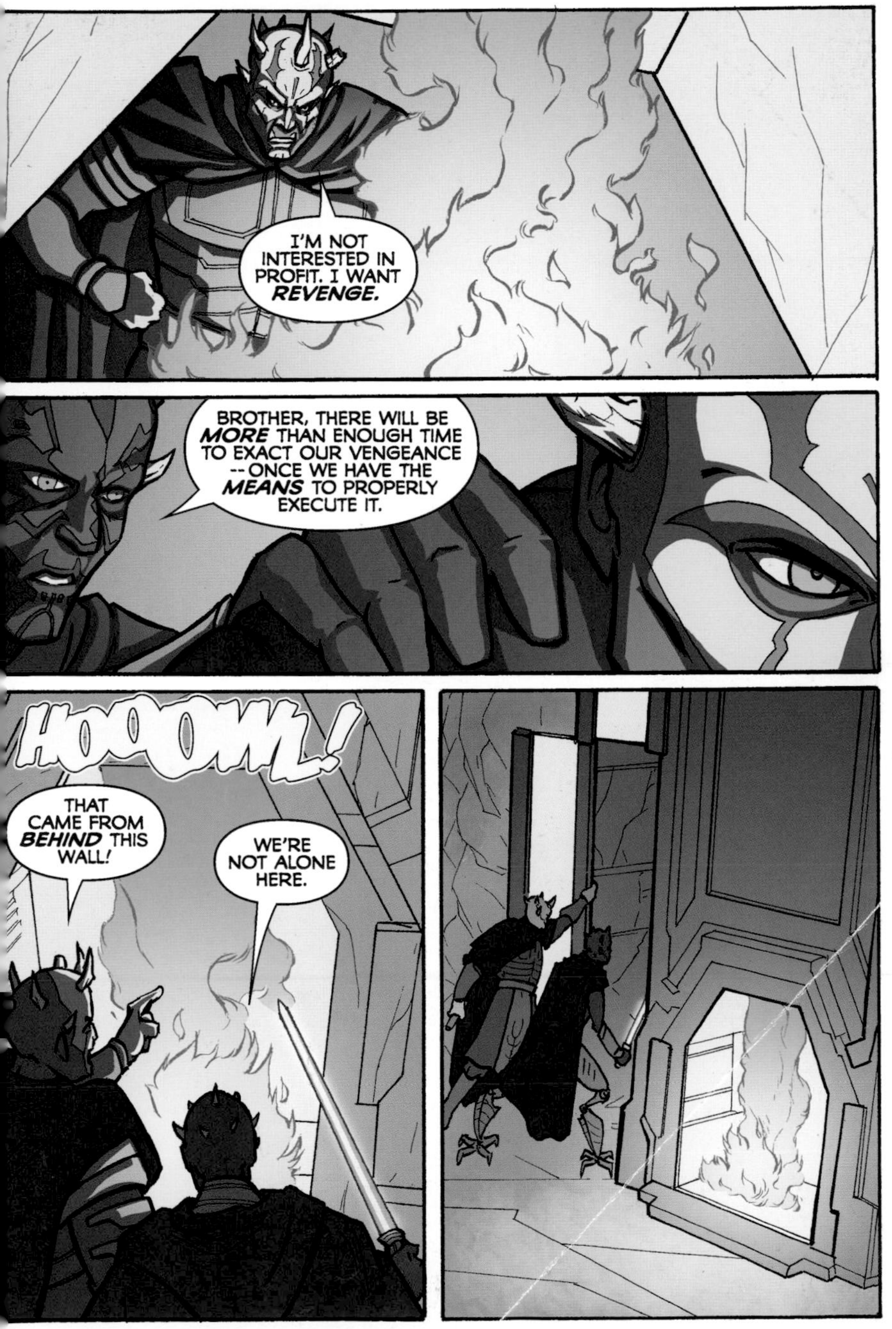
I'M NOT INTERESTED IN PROFIT. I WANT *REVENGE.*
BROTHER, THERE WILL BE *MORE* THAN ENOUGH TIME TO EXACT OUR VENGEANCE --ONCE WE HAVE THE *MEANS* TO PROPERLY EXECUTE IT.
HOOOWL!
THAT CAME FROM *BEHIND* THIS WALL!
WE'RE NOT ALONE HERE.

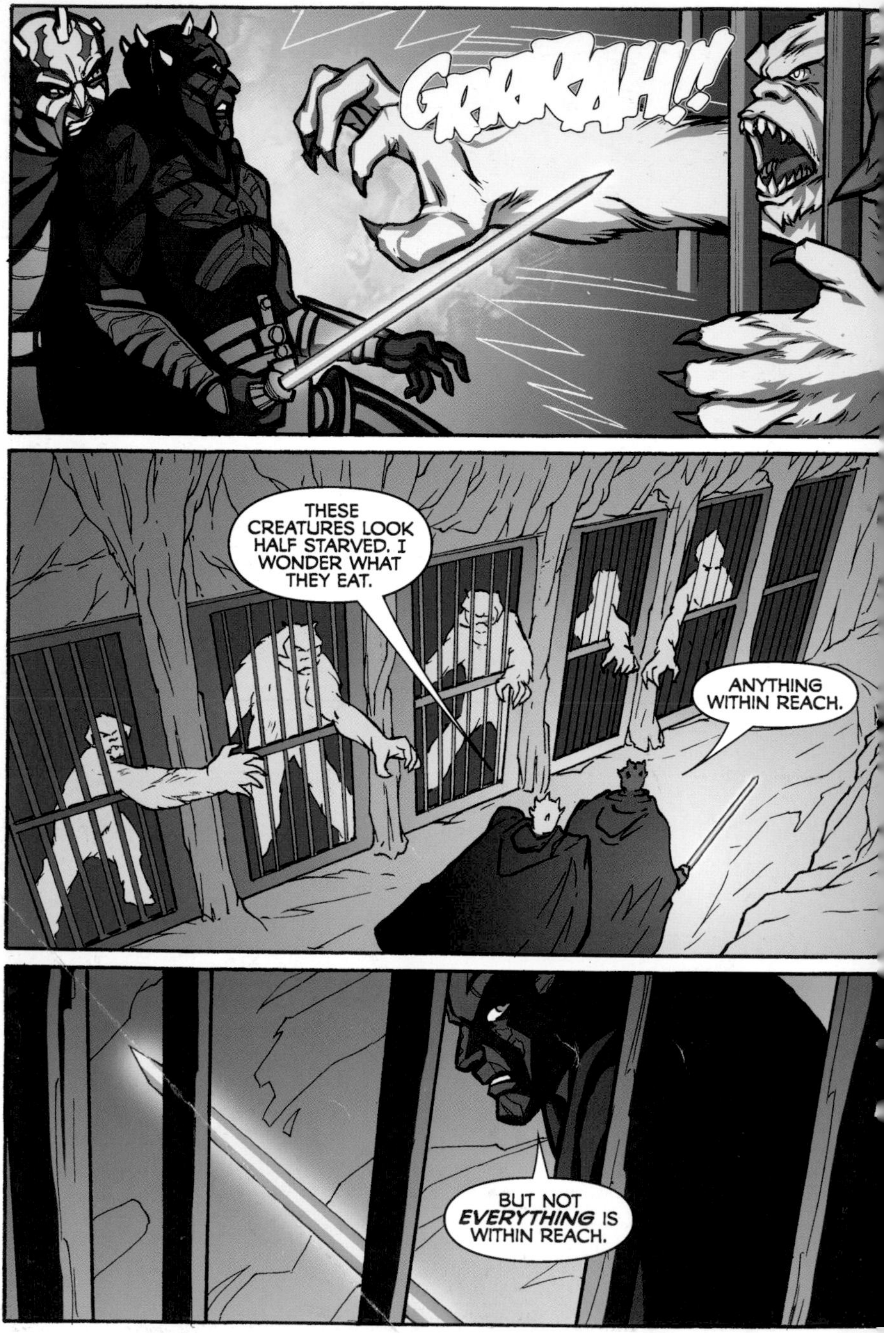
GRRRAAH!!
THESE CREATURES LOOK HALF STARVED. I WONDER WHAT THEY EAT.
ANYTHING WITHIN REACH.
BUT NOT *EVERYTHING* IS WITHIN REACH.

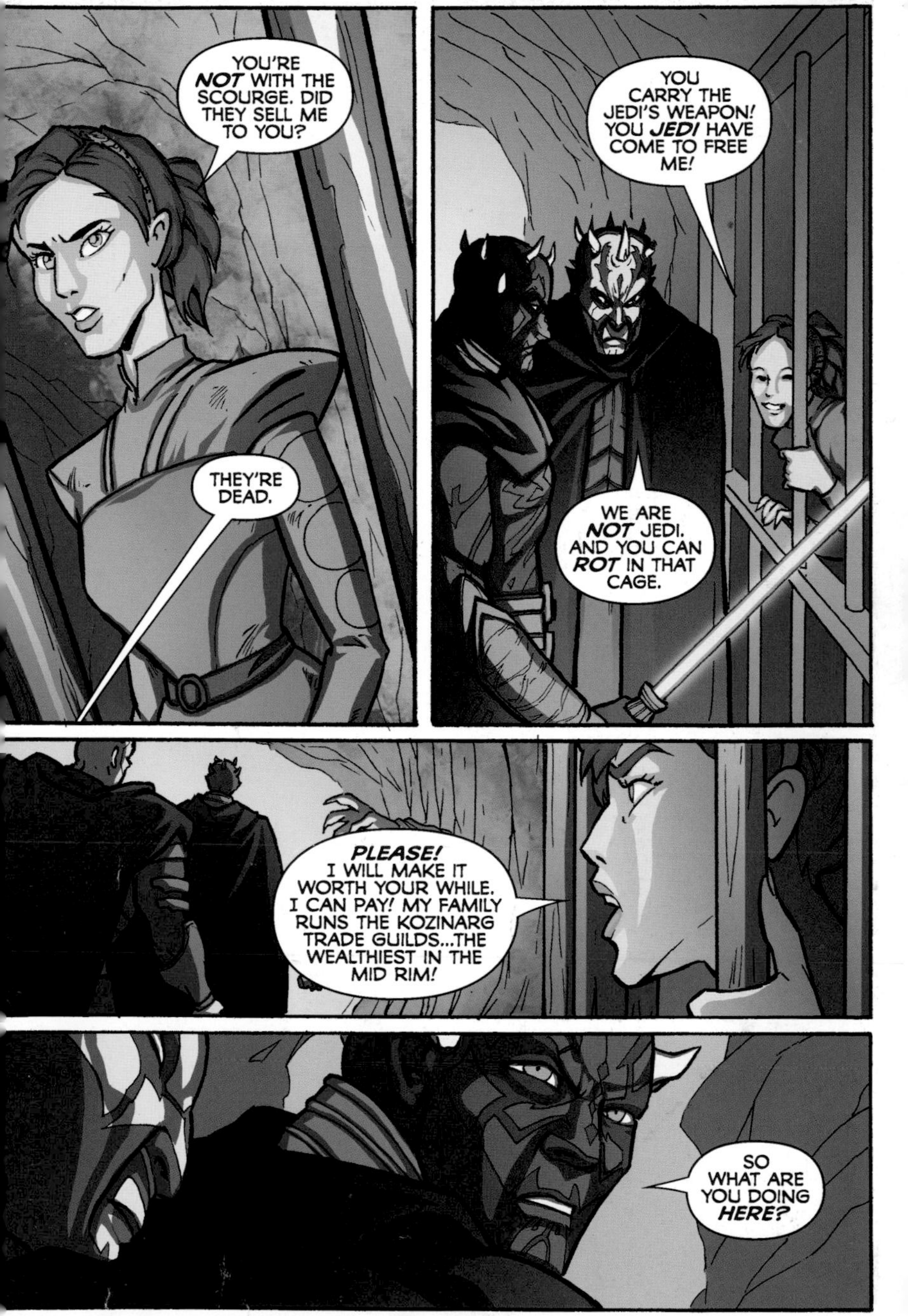
YOU'RE NOT WITH THE SCOURGE. DID THEY SELL ME TO YOU?
THEY'RE DEAD.
YOU CARRY THE JEDI'S WEAPON! YOU JEDI HAVE COME TO FREE ME!
WE ARE NOT JEDI. AND YOU CAN ROT IN THAT CAGE.
PLEASE! I WILL MAKE IT WORTH YOUR WHILE. I CAN PAY! MY FAMILY RUNS THE KOZINARG TRADE GUILDS...THE WEALTHIEST IN THE MID RIM!
SO WHAT ARE YOU DOING HERE?

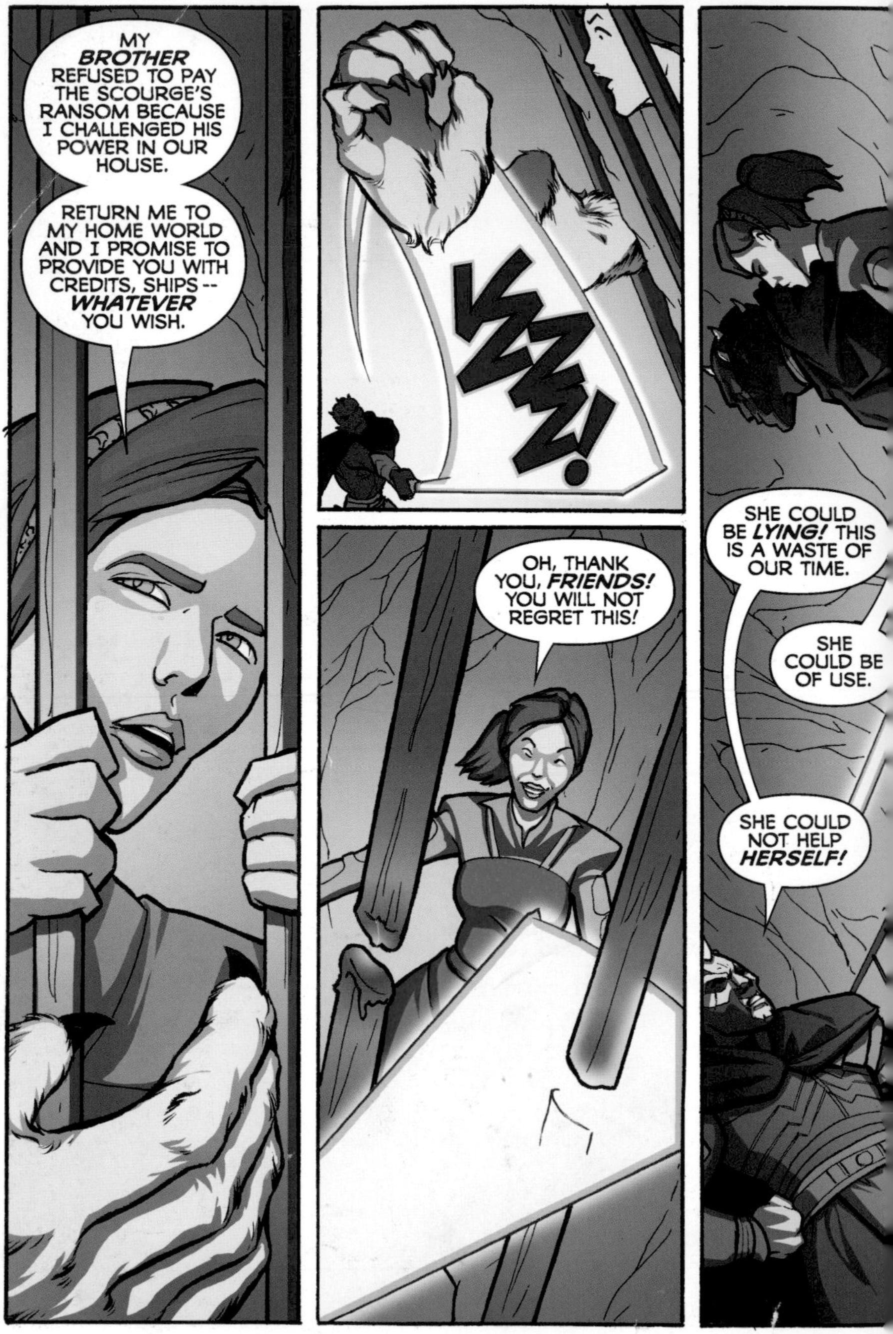
MY BROTHER REFUSED TO PAY THE SCOURGE'S RANSOM BECAUSE I CHALLENGED HIS POWER IN OUR HOUSE.
RETURN ME TO MY HOME WORLD AND I PROMISE TO PROVIDE YOU WITH CREDITS, SHIPS -- WHATEVER YOU WISH.
VVVV!
OH, THANK YOU, FRIENDS! YOU WILL NOT REGRET THIS!
SHE COULD BE LYING! THIS IS A WASTE OF OUR TIME.
SHE COULD BE OF USE.
SHE COULD NOT HELP HERSELF!

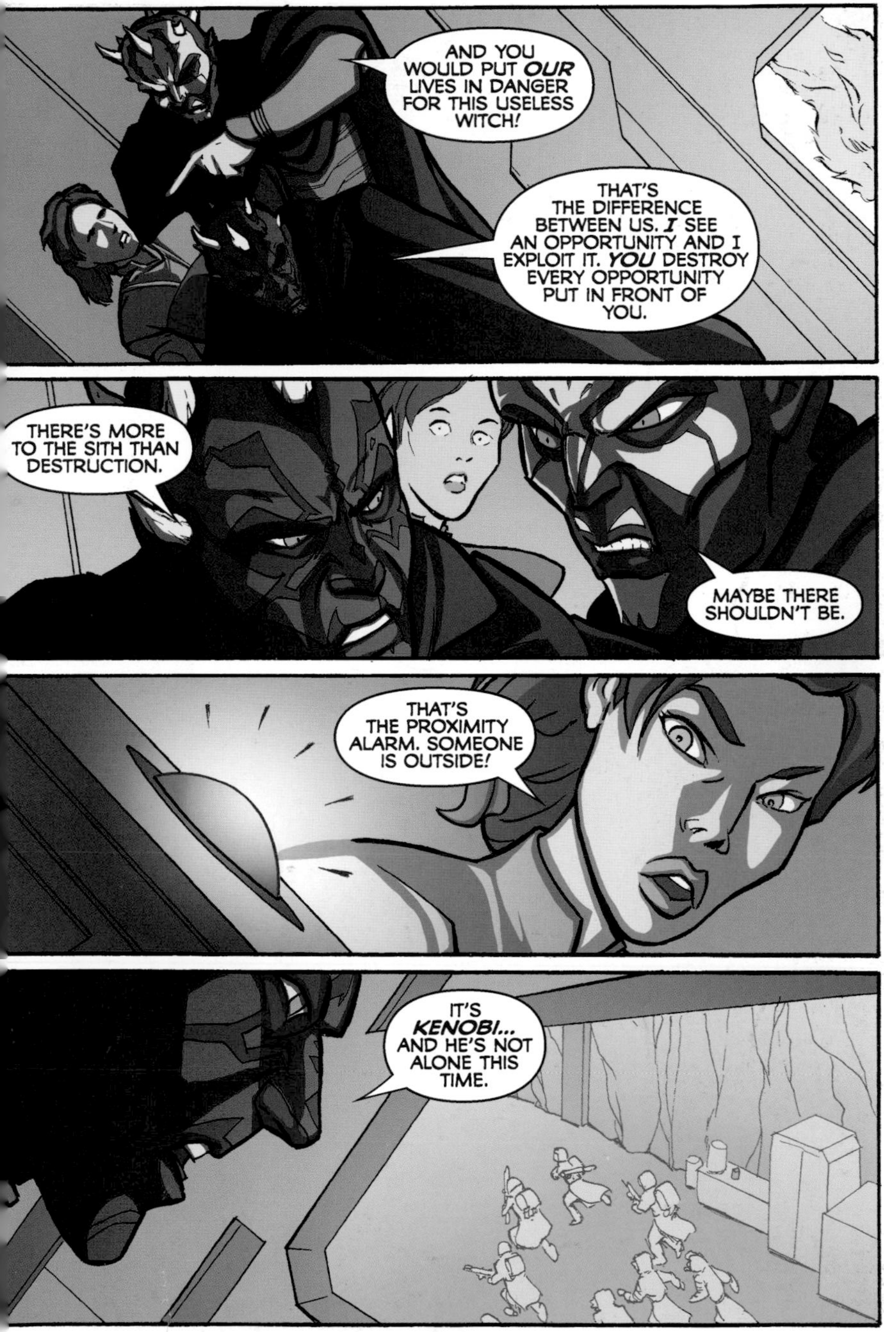
AND YOU WOULD PUT *OUR* LIVES IN DANGER FOR THIS USELESS WITCH!
THAT'S THE DIFFERENCE BETWEEN US. *I* SEE AN OPPORTUNITY AND I EXPLOIT IT. *YOU* DESTROY EVERY OPPORTUNITY PUT IN FRONT OF YOU.
THERE'S MORE TO THE SITH THAN DESTRUCTION.
MAYBE THERE SHOULDN'T BE.
THAT'S THE PROXIMITY ALARM. SOMEONE IS OUTSIDE!
IT'S *KENOBI*... AND HE'S NOT ALONE THIS TIME.

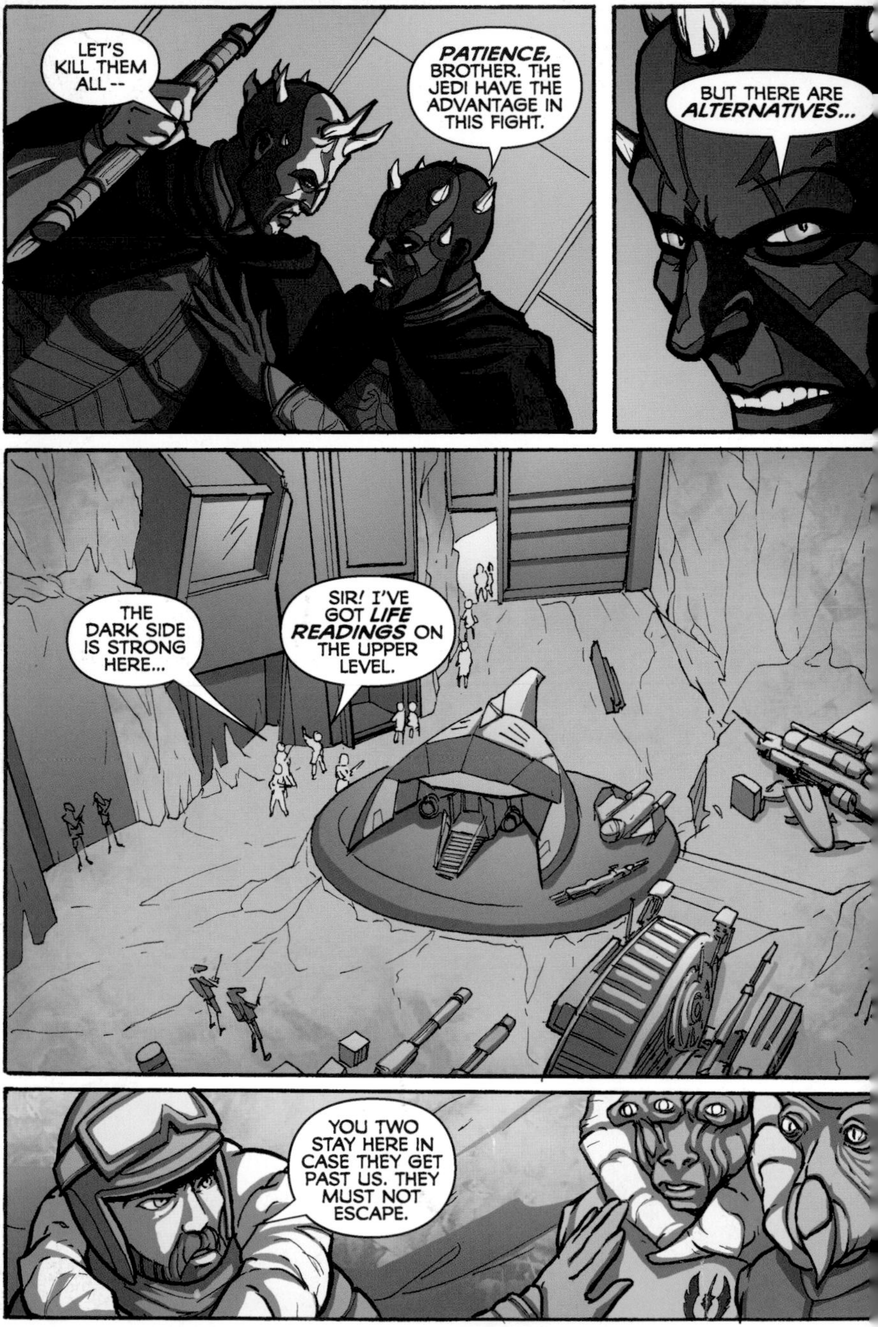
LET'S KILL THEM ALL --
PATIENCE, BROTHER. THE JEDI HAVE THE ADVANTAGE IN THIS FIGHT.
BUT THERE ARE ALTERNATIVES...
THE DARK SIDE IS STRONG HERE...
SIR! I'VE GOT LIFE READINGS ON THE UPPER LEVEL.
YOU TWO STAY HERE IN CASE THEY GET PAST US. THEY MUST NOT ESCAPE.

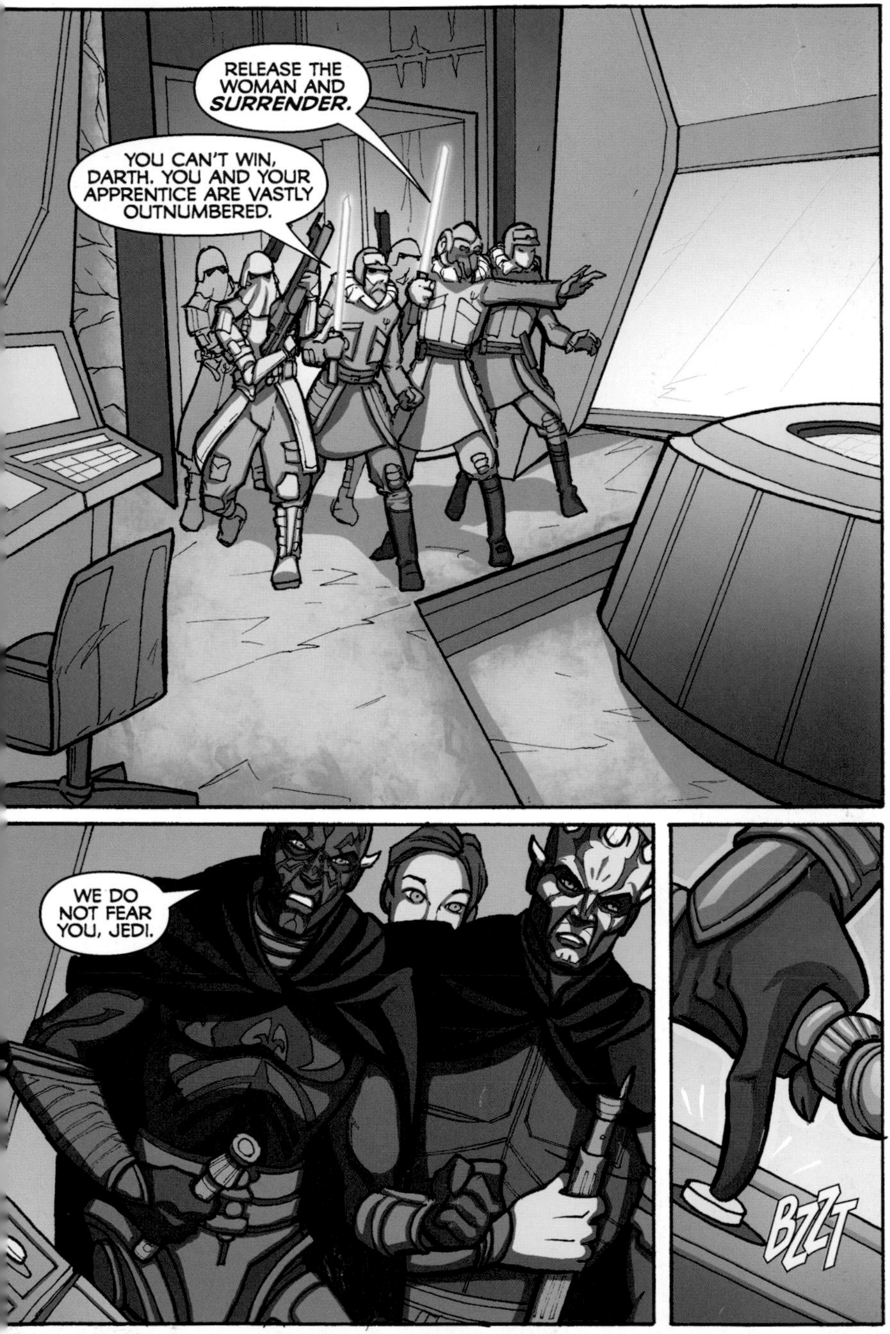
RELEASE THE WOMAN AND SURRENDER.
YOU CAN'T WIN, DARTH. YOU AND YOUR APPRENTICE ARE VASTLY OUTNUMBERED.
WE DO NOT FEAR YOU, JEDI.
BZZT

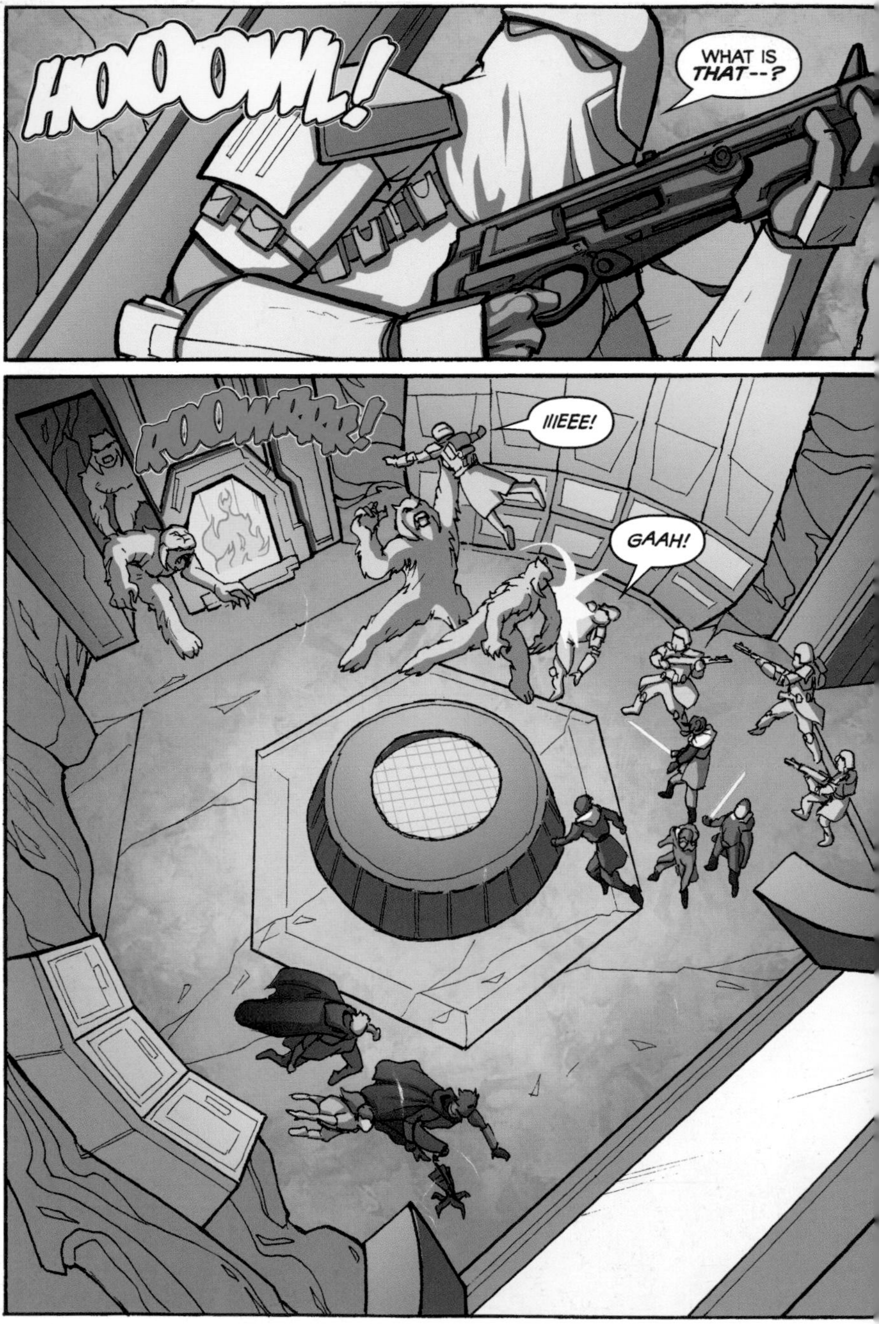
HOOOOWL!
WHAT IS THAT--?
ROOWRRR!
IIIEEE!
GAAH!

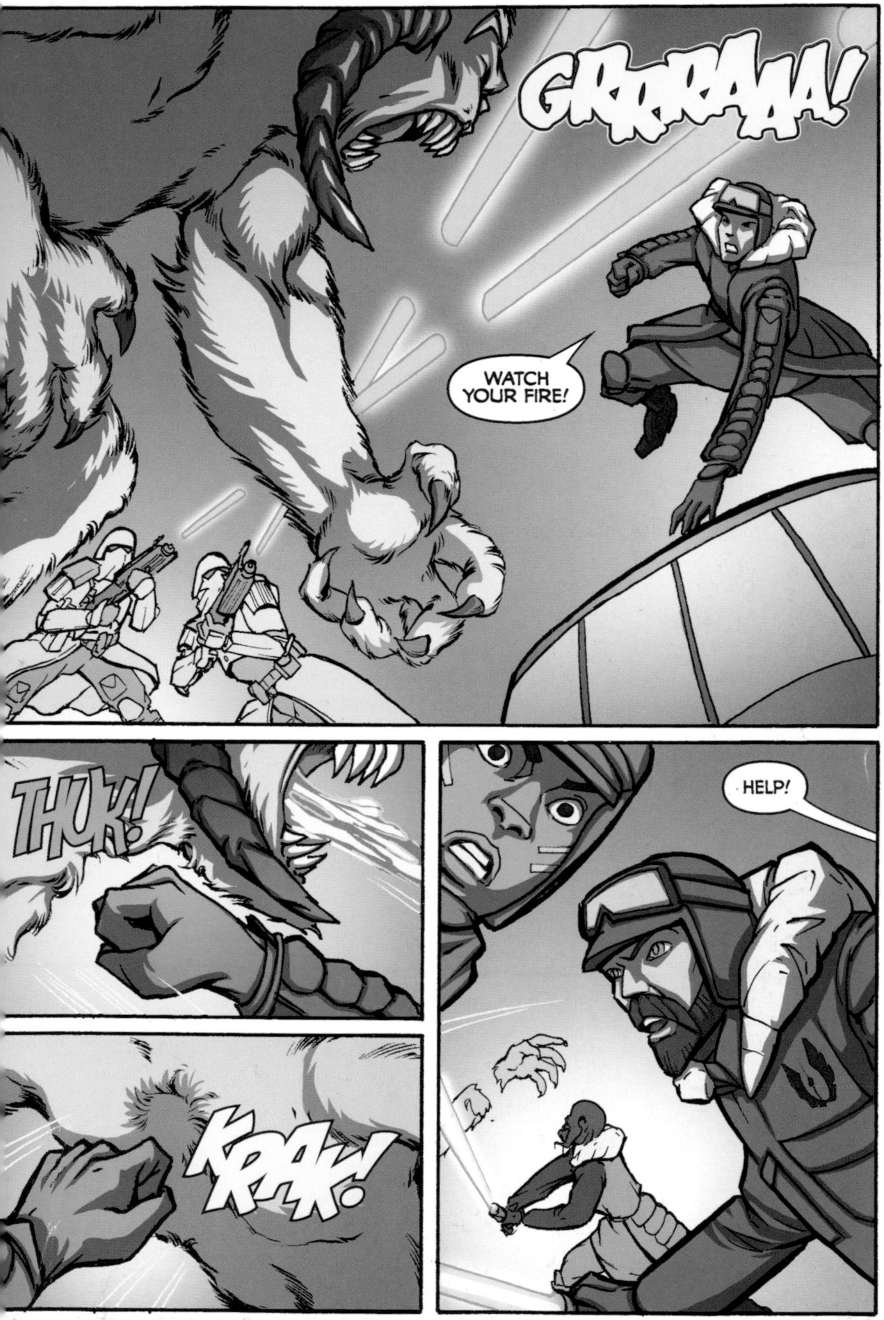
GRRRAAA!
WATCH YOUR FIRE!
THUK!
KRAK!
HELP!

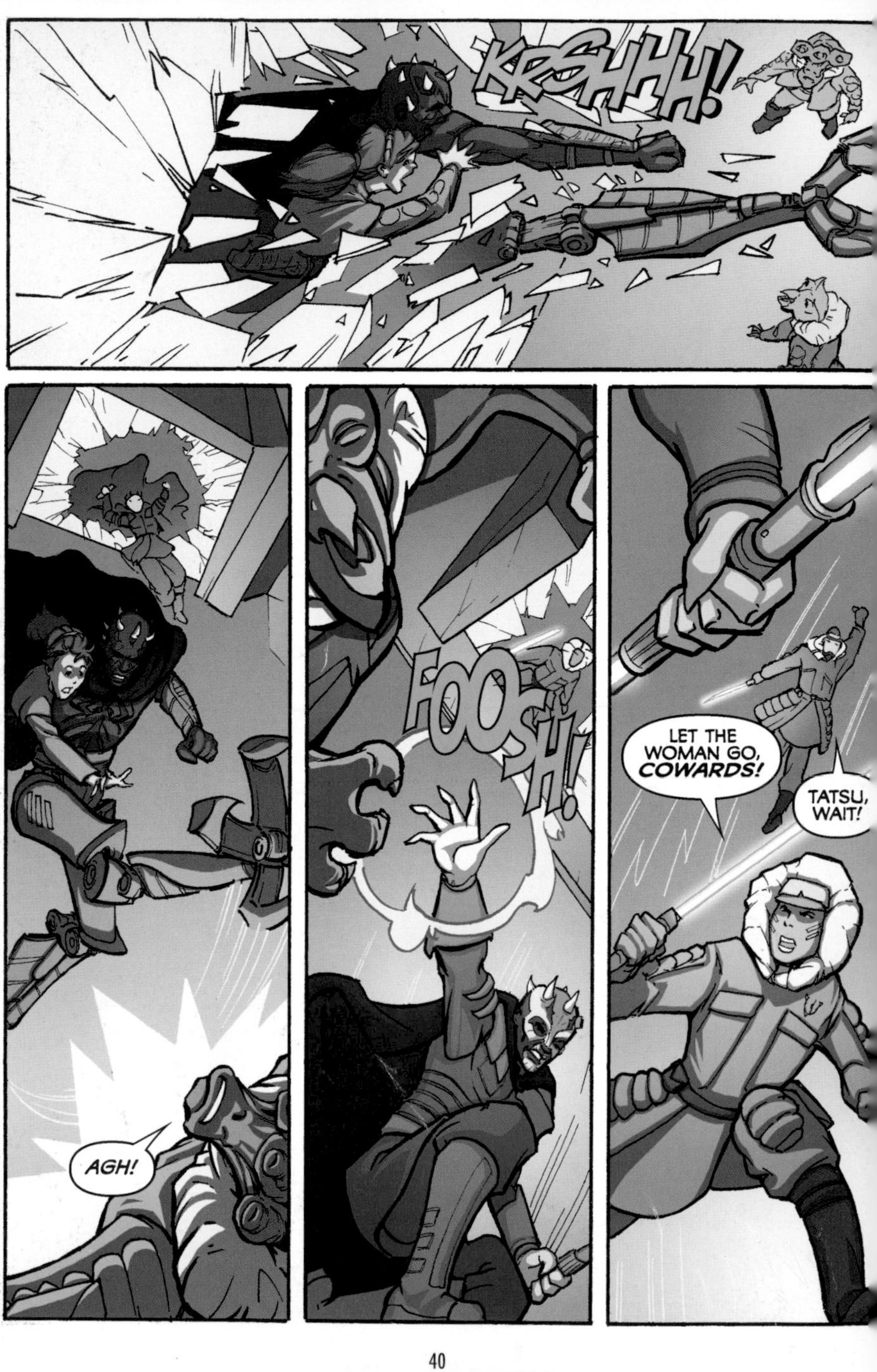
KRSHHH!
AGH!
FOOSH!
LET THE WOMAN GO, COWARDS!
TATSU, WAIT!

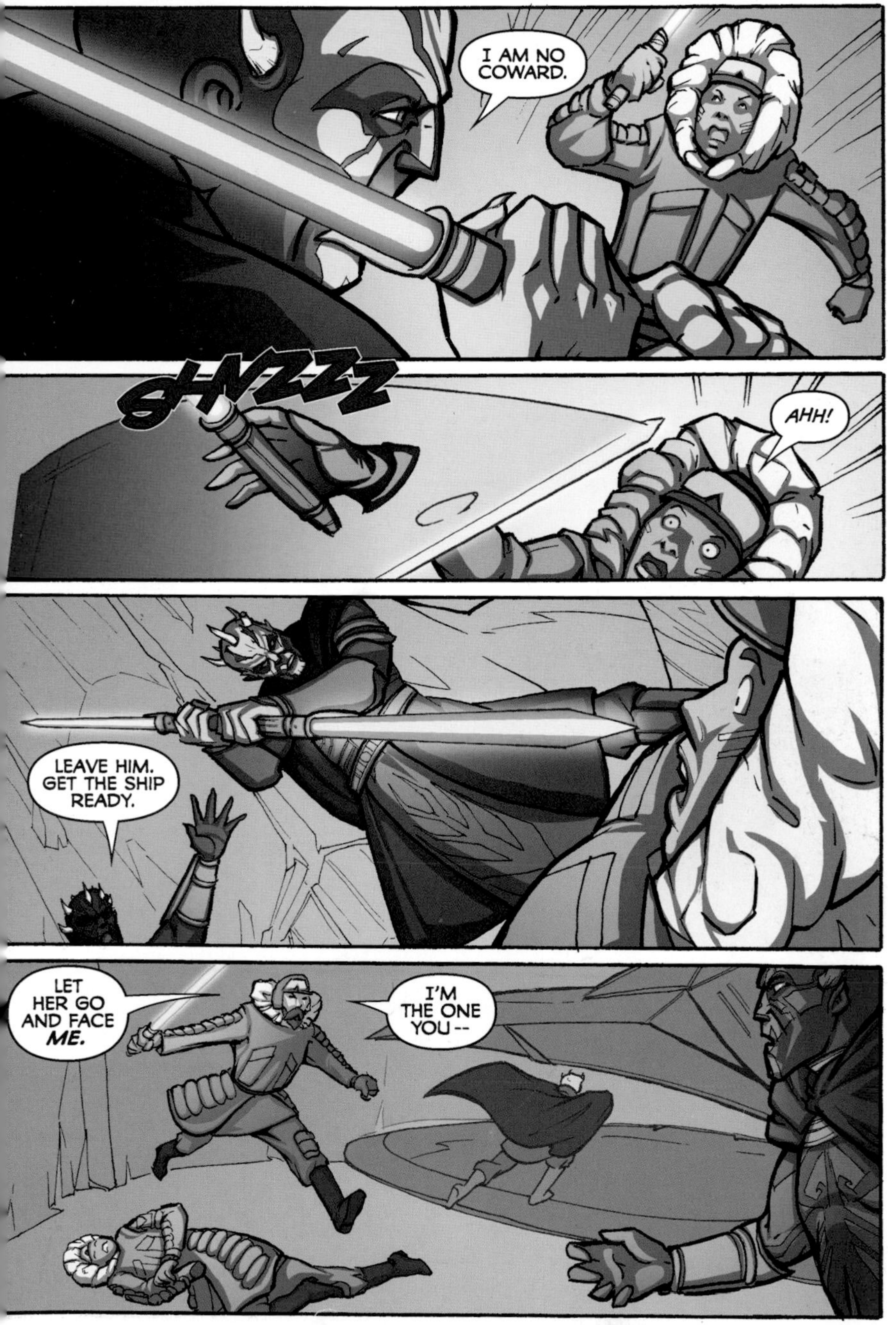
I AM NO COWARD.
SHNZZZ
AHH!
LEAVE HIM. GET THE SHIP READY.
LET HER GO AND FACE *ME.*
I'M THE ONE YOU --

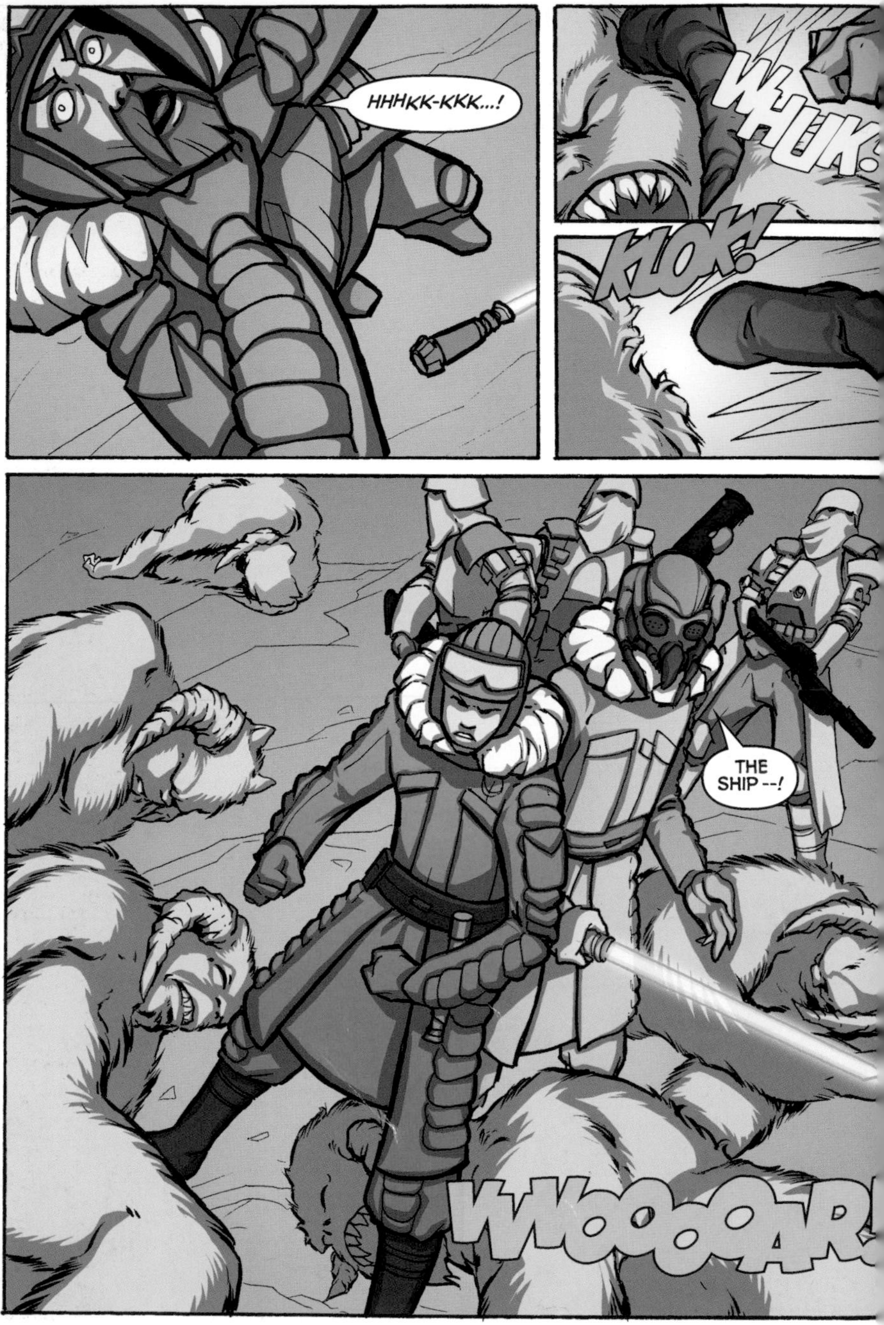
HHHKK-KKK...!
WHUK!
KLOK!
THE SHIP --!
WHOOOOAR!

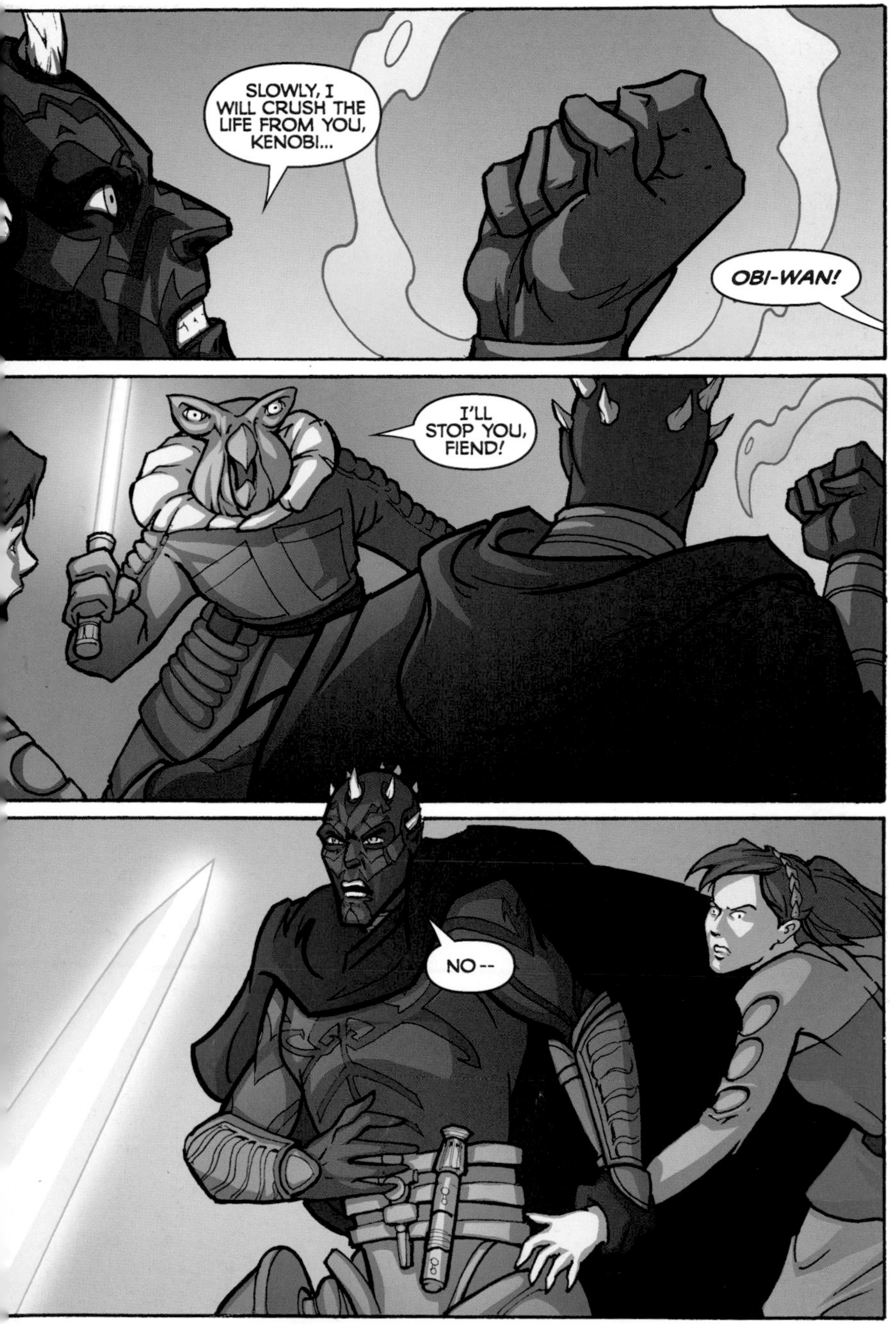
SLOWLY, I WILL CRUSH THE LIFE FROM YOU, KENOBI...
OBI-WAN!
I'LL STOP YOU, FIEND!
NO--

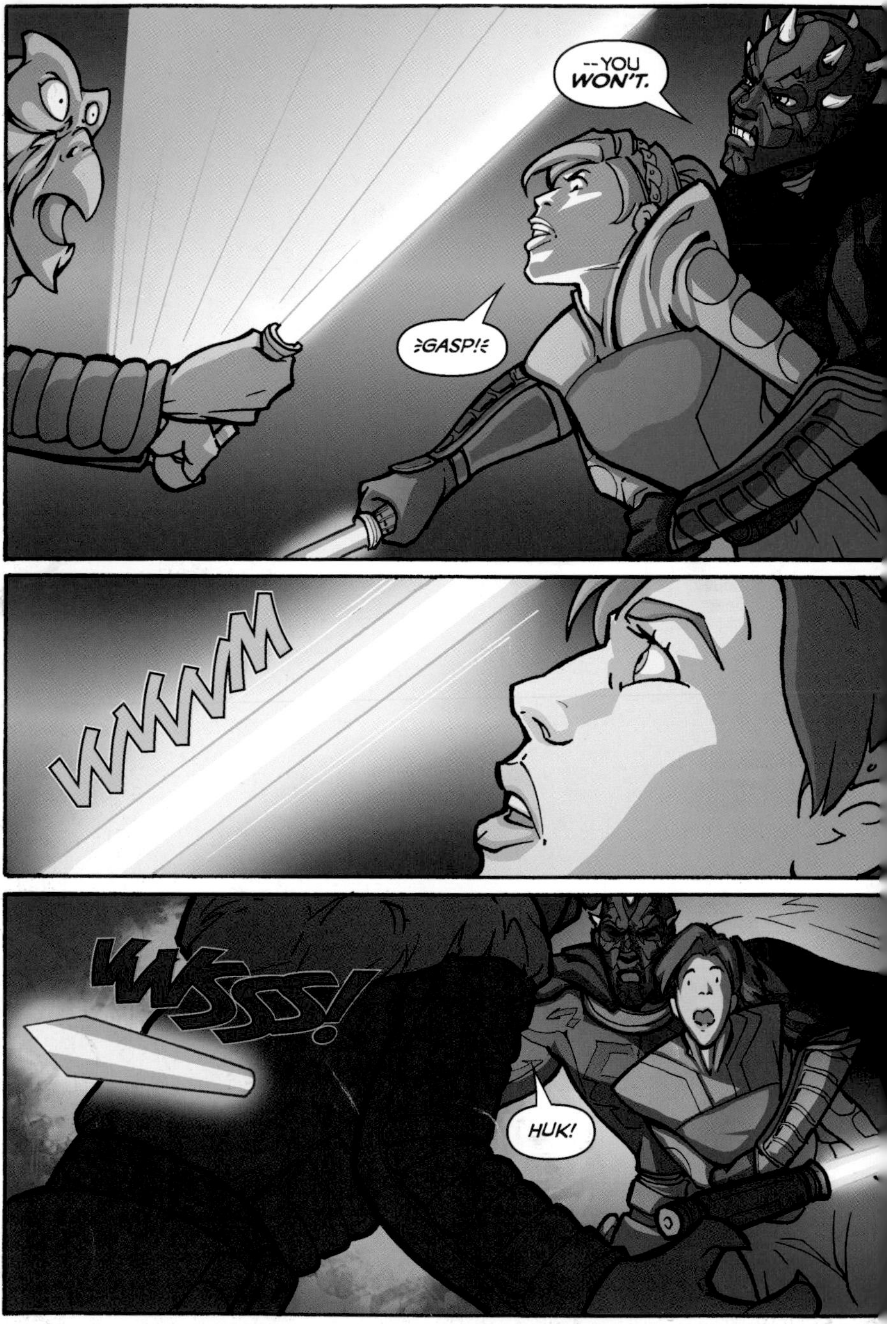
--YOU WON'T.
GASP!
WMMM
WSSS!
HUK!

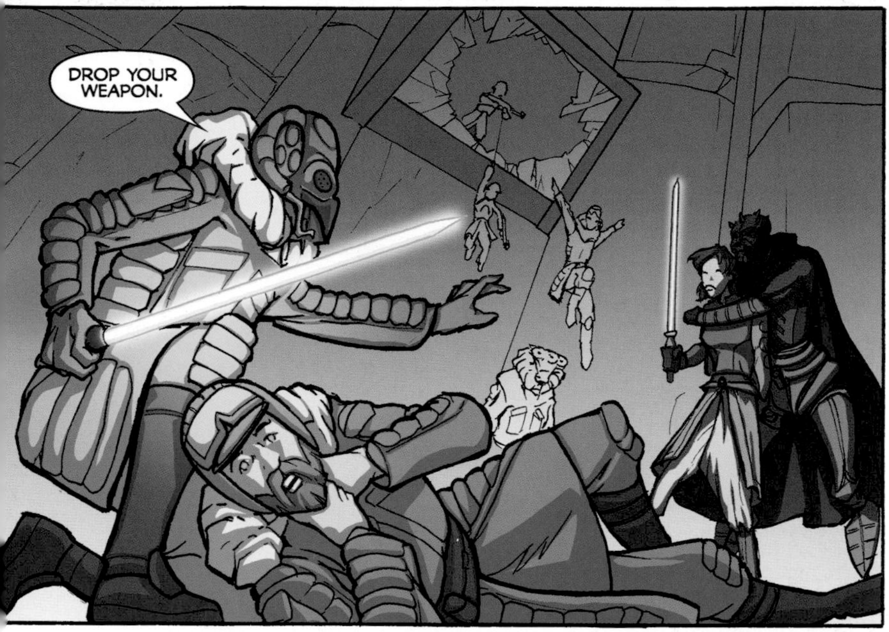
DROP YOUR WEAPON.

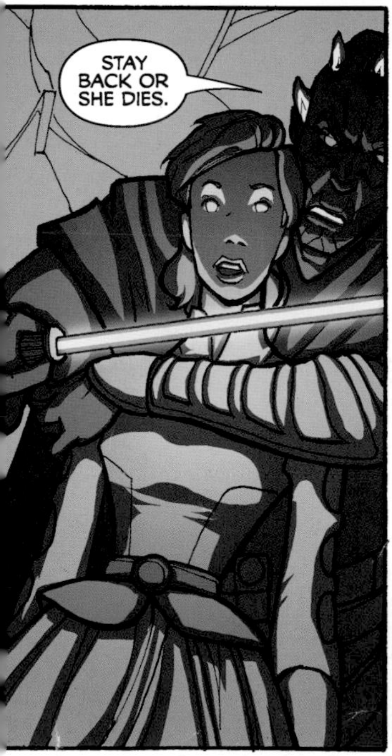
STAY BACK OR SHE DIES.

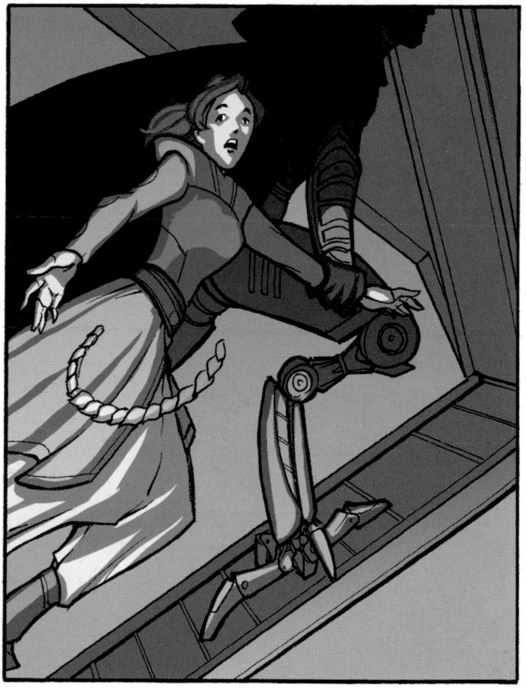

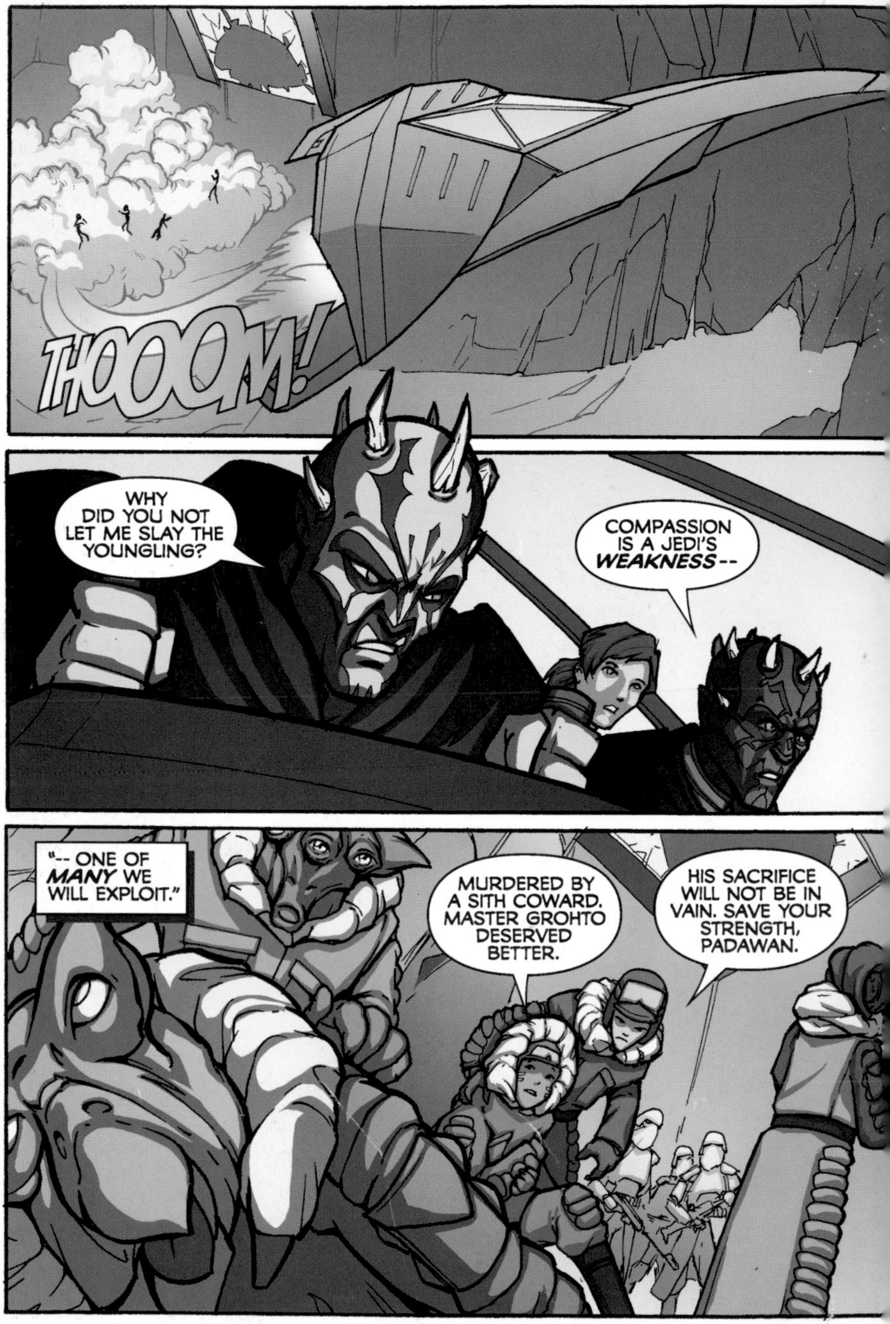
THOOOM!
WHY DID YOU NOT LET ME SLAY THE YOUNGLING?
COMPASSION IS A JEDI'S *WEAKNESS* --
"-- ONE OF *MANY* WE WILL EXPLOIT."
MURDERED BY A SITH COWARD. MASTER GROHTO DESERVED BETTER.
HIS SACRIFICE WILL NOT BE IN VAIN. SAVE YOUR STRENGTH, PADAWAN.

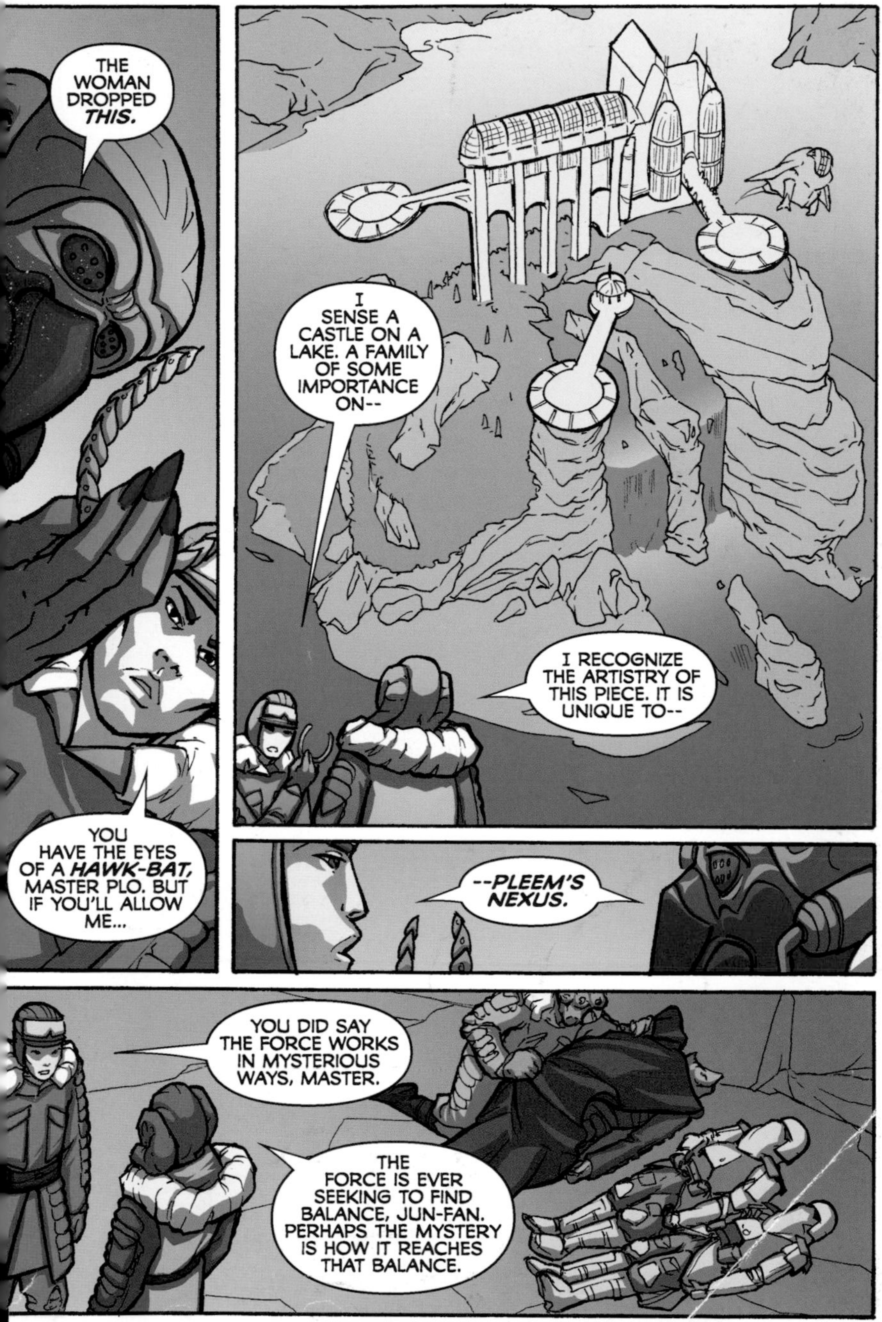
THE WOMAN DROPPED *THIS.*
YOU HAVE THE EYES OF A *HAWK-BAT,* MASTER PLO. BUT IF YOU'LL ALLOW ME...
I SENSE A CASTLE ON A LAKE. A FAMILY OF SOME IMPORTANCE ON--
I RECOGNIZE THE ARTISTRY OF THIS PIECE. IT IS UNIQUE TO--
--PLEEM'S NEXUS.
YOU DID SAY THE FORCE WORKS IN MYSTERIOUS WAYS, MASTER.
THE FORCE IS EVER SEEKING TO FIND BALANCE, JUN-FAN. PERHAPS THE MYSTERY IS HOW IT REACHES THAT BALANCE.

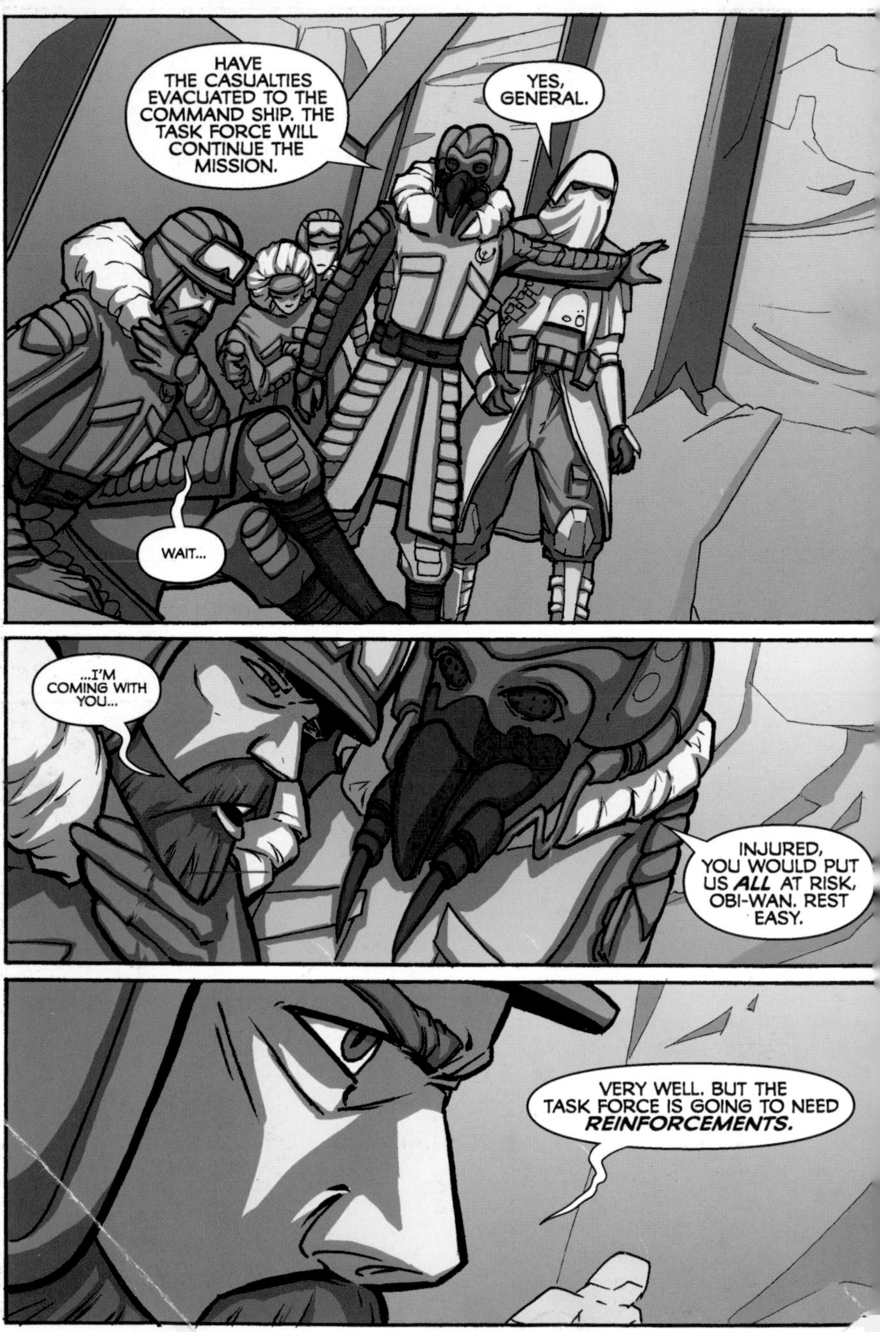
HAVE THE CASUALTIES EVACUATED TO THE COMMAND SHIP. THE TASK FORCE WILL CONTINUE THE MISSION.
YES, GENERAL.
WAIT...
...I'M COMING WITH YOU...
INJURED, YOU WOULD PUT US *ALL* AT RISK, OBI-WAN. REST EASY.
VERY WELL. BUT THE TASK FORCE IS GOING TO NEED ***REINFORCEMENTS.***

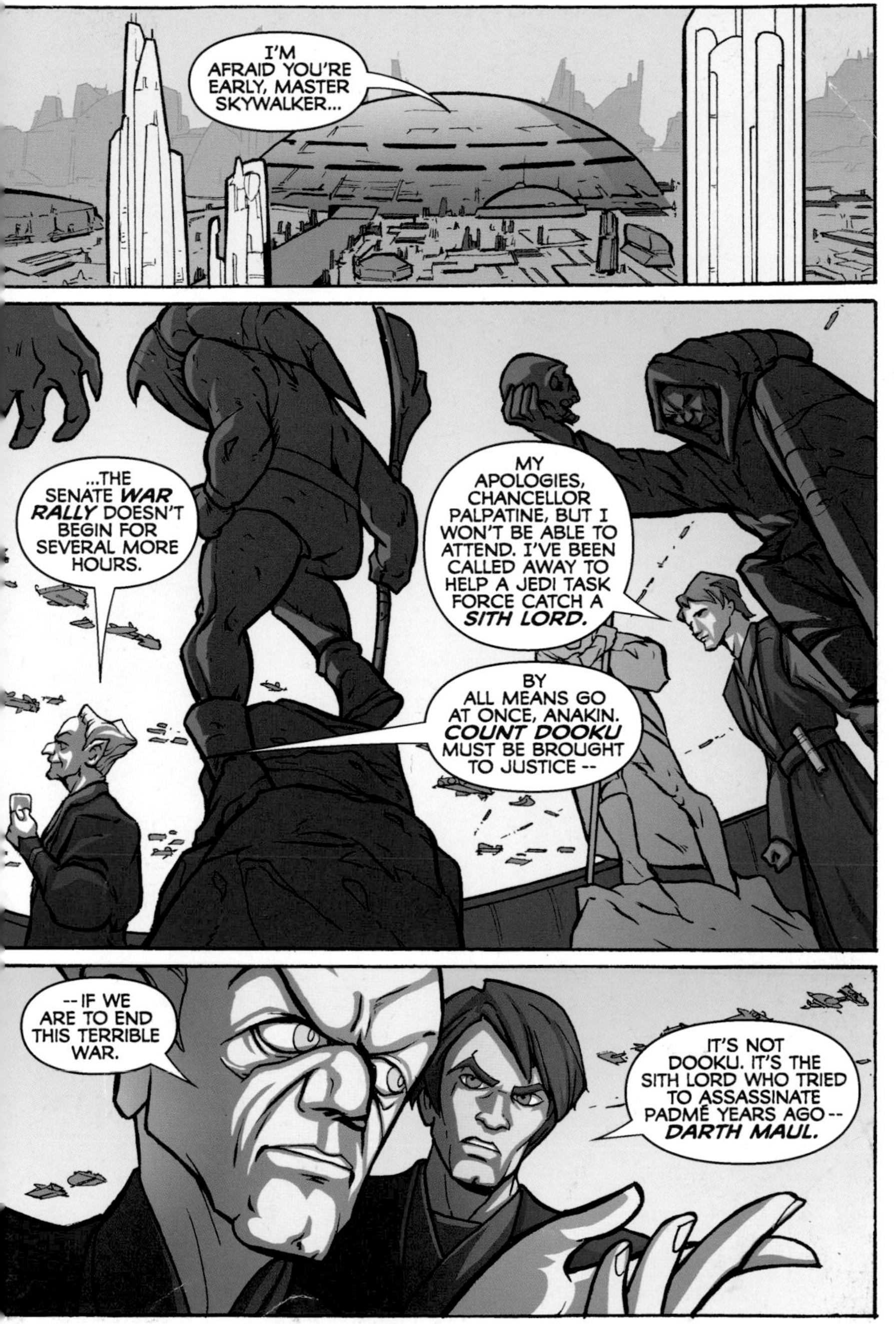

I'M AFRAID YOU'RE EARLY, MASTER SKYWALKER...
...THE SENATE *WAR RALLY* DOESN'T BEGIN FOR SEVERAL MORE HOURS.
MY APOLOGIES, CHANCELLOR PALPATINE, BUT I WON'T BE ABLE TO ATTEND. I'VE BEEN CALLED AWAY TO HELP A JEDI TASK FORCE CATCH A *SITH LORD.*
BY ALL MEANS GO AT ONCE, ANAKIN. *COUNT DOOKU* MUST BE BROUGHT TO JUSTICE --
-- IF WE ARE TO END THIS TERRIBLE WAR.
IT'S NOT DOOKU. IT'S THE SITH LORD WHO TRIED TO ASSASSINATE PADMÉ YEARS AGO -- *DARTH MAUL.*

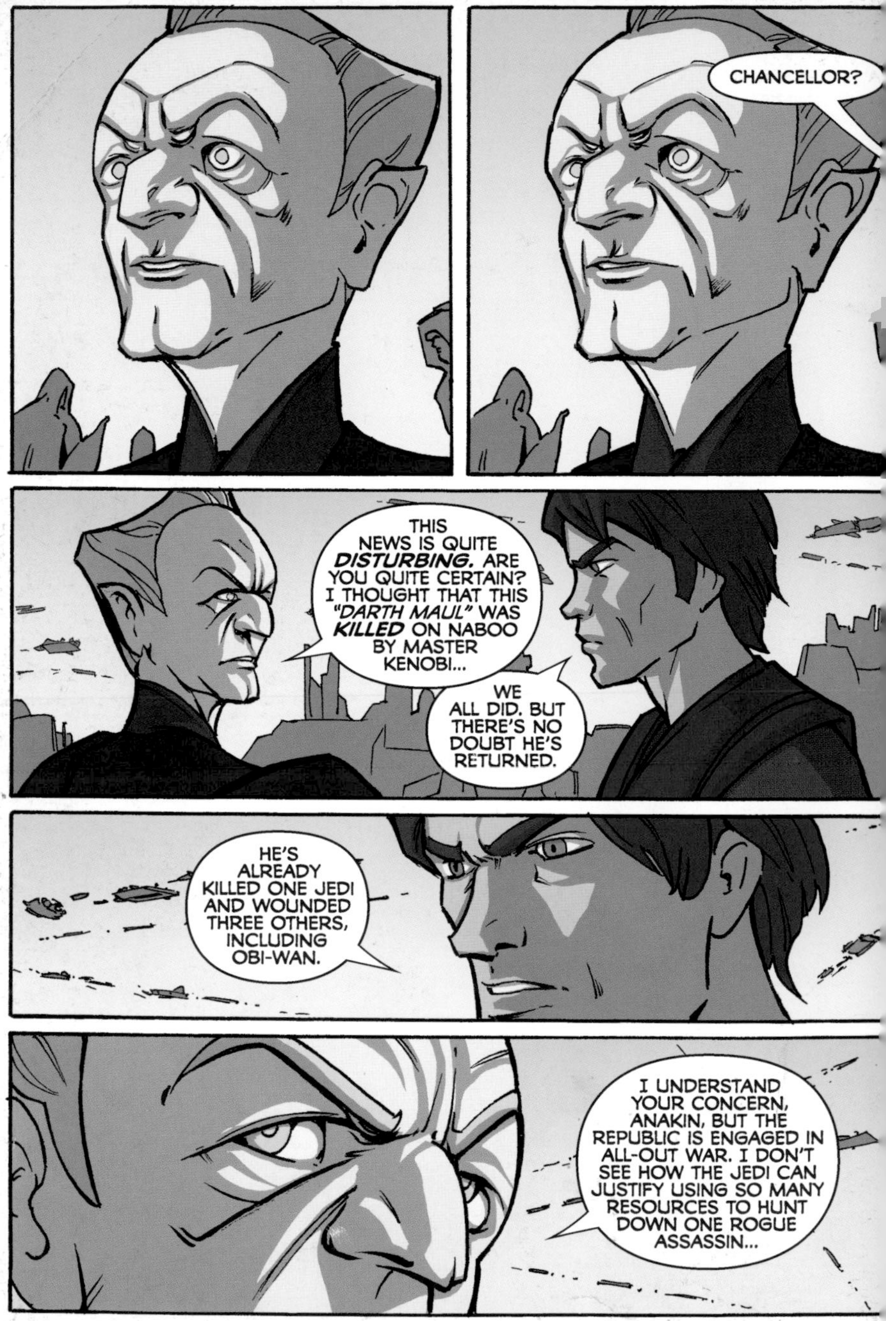
CHANCELLOR?
THIS NEWS IS QUITE *DISTURBING.* ARE YOU QUITE CERTAIN? I THOUGHT THAT THIS "*DARTH MAUL*" WAS *KILLED* ON NABOO BY MASTER KENOBI...
WE ALL DID. BUT THERE'S NO DOUBT HE'S RETURNED.
HE'S ALREADY KILLED ONE JEDI AND WOUNDED THREE OTHERS, INCLUDING OBI-WAN.
I UNDERSTAND YOUR CONCERN, ANAKIN, BUT THE REPUBLIC IS ENGAGED IN ALL-OUT WAR. I DON'T SEE HOW THE JEDI CAN JUSTIFY USING SO MANY RESOURCES TO HUNT DOWN ONE ROGUE ASSASSIN...

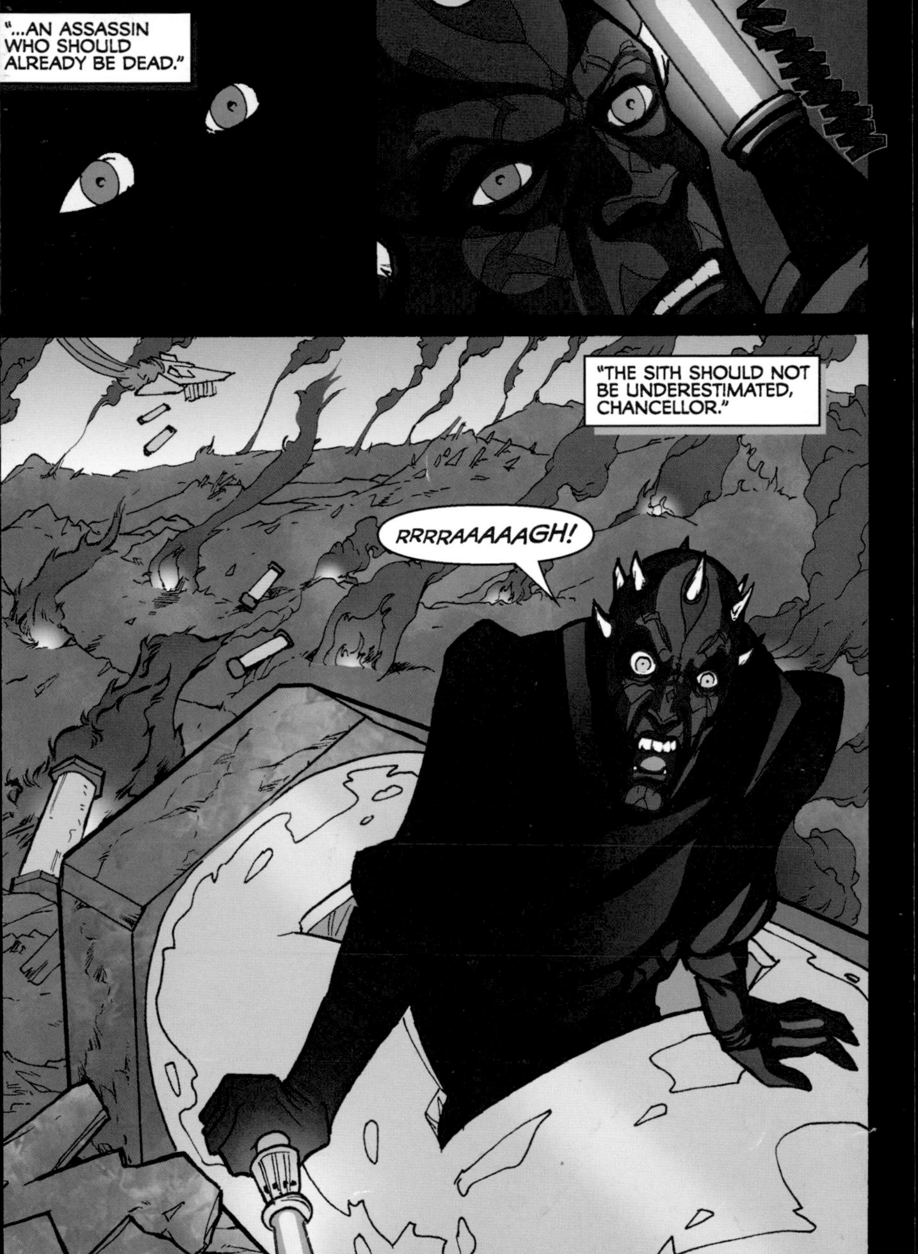
"...AN ASSASSIN WHO SHOULD ALREADY BE DEAD."
"THE SITH SHOULD NOT BE UNDERESTIMATED, CHANCELLOR."
RRRRAAAAAGH!

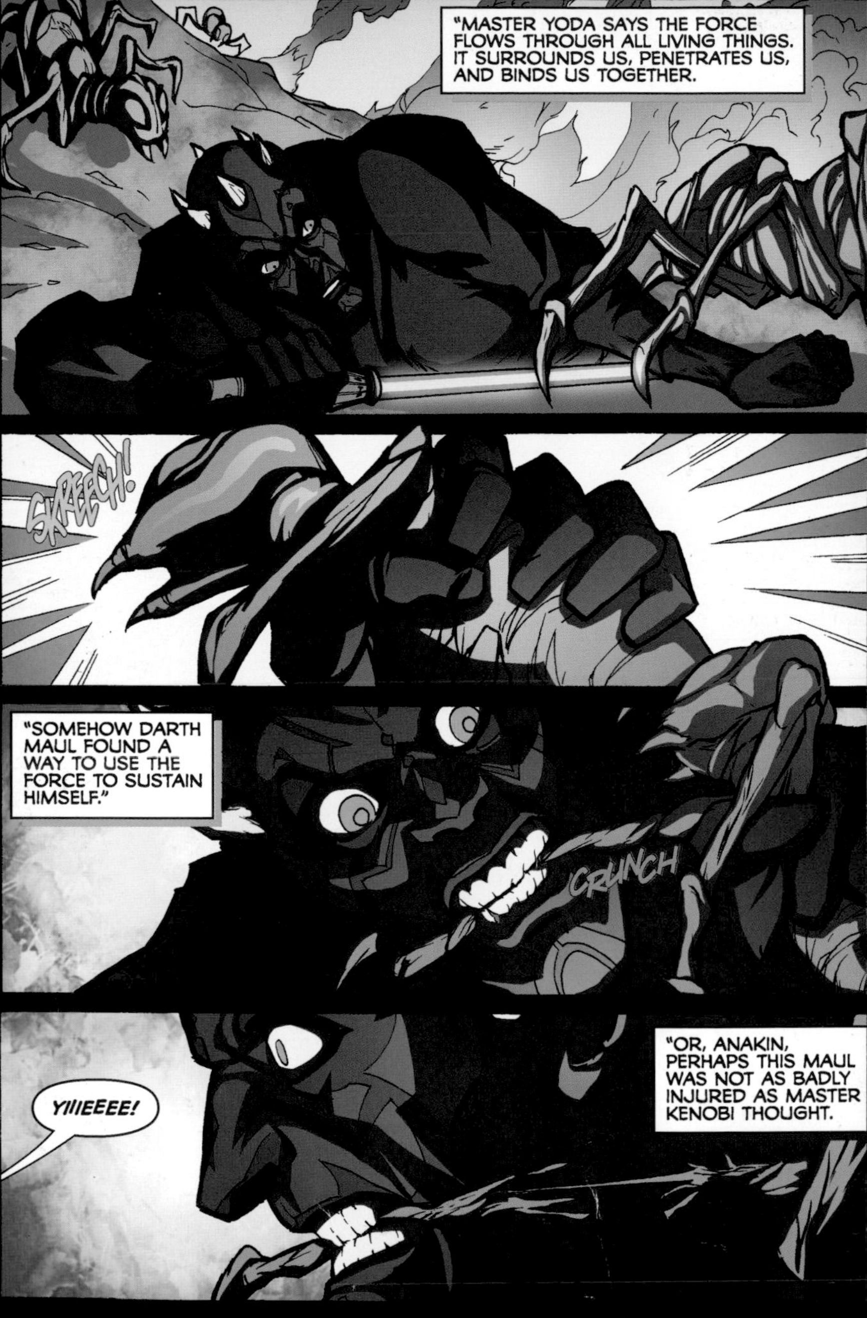
"MASTER YODA SAYS THE FORCE FLOWS THROUGH ALL LIVING THINGS. IT SURROUNDS US, PENETRATES US, AND BINDS US TOGETHER.
SKREECH!
"SOMEHOW DARTH MAUL FOUND A WAY TO USE THE FORCE TO SUSTAIN HIMSELF."
CRUNCH
YIIIEEEE!
"OR, ANAKIN, PERHAPS THIS MAUL WAS NOT AS BADLY INJURED AS MASTER KENOBI THOUGHT.

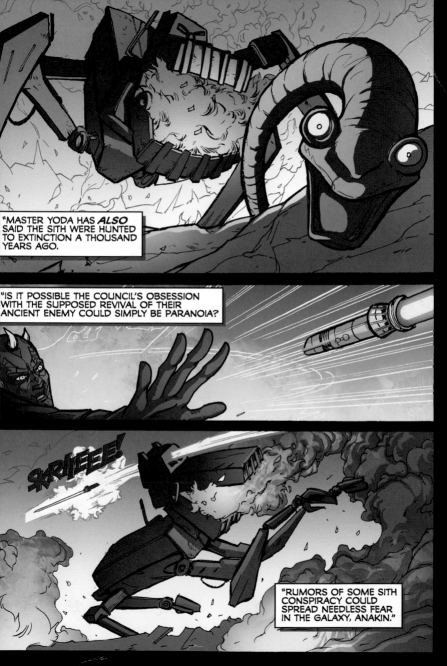

"MASTER YODA HAS *ALSO* SAID THE SITH WERE HUNTED TO EXTINCTION A THOUSAND YEARS AGO.

"IS IT POSSIBLE THE COUNCIL'S OBSESSION WITH THE SUPPOSED REVIVAL OF THEIR ANCIENT ENEMY COULD SIMPLY BE PARANOIA?

SKRIIEEE!

"RUMORS OF SOME SITH CONSPIRACY COULD SPREAD NEEDLESS FEAR IN THE GALAXY, ANAKIN."

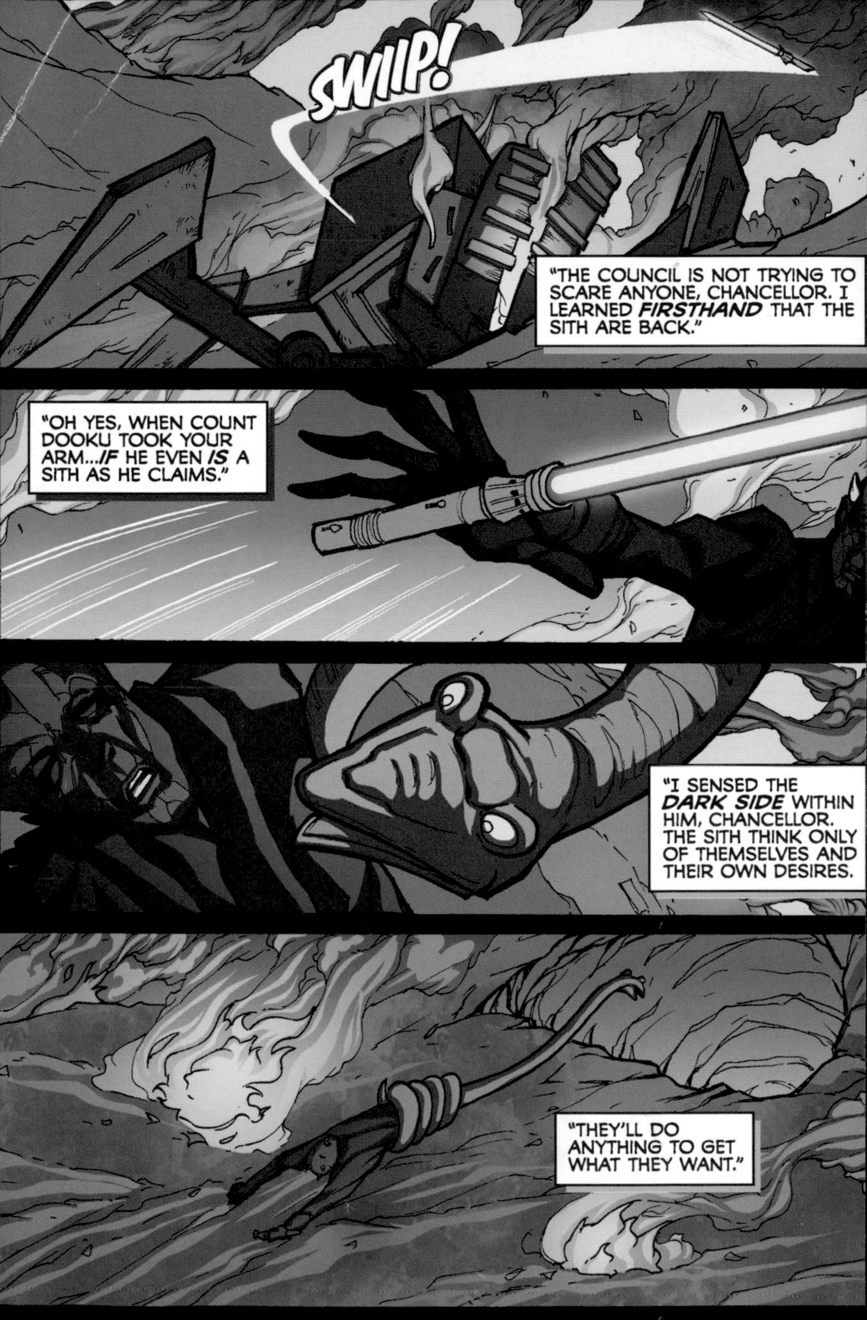
SWIIP!
"THE COUNCIL IS NOT TRYING TO SCARE ANYONE, CHANCELLOR. I LEARNED FIRSTHAND THAT THE SITH ARE BACK."
"OH YES, WHEN COUNT DOOKU TOOK YOUR ARM...IF HE EVEN IS A SITH AS HE CLAIMS."
"I SENSED THE DARK SIDE WITHIN HIM, CHANCELLOR. THE SITH THINK ONLY OF THEMSELVES AND THEIR OWN DESIRES.
"THEY'LL DO ANYTHING TO GET WHAT THEY WANT."

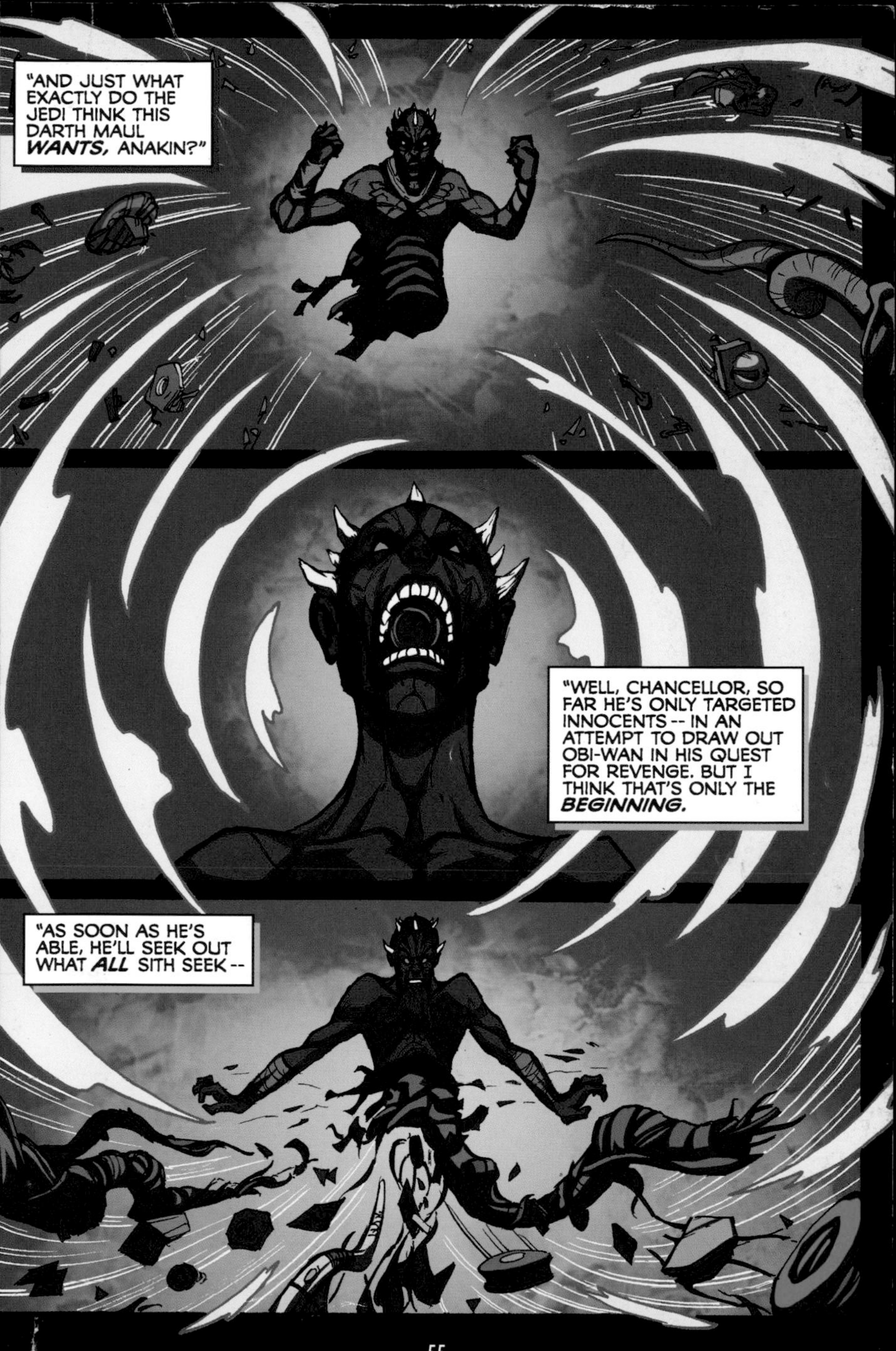
"AND JUST WHAT EXACTLY DO THE JEDI THINK THIS DARTH MAUL *WANTS,* ANAKIN?"
"WELL, CHANCELLOR, SO FAR HE'S ONLY TARGETED INNOCENTS -- IN AN ATTEMPT TO DRAW OUT OBI-WAN IN HIS QUEST FOR REVENGE. BUT I THINK THAT'S ONLY THE *BEGINNING.*
"AS SOON AS HE'S ABLE, HE'LL SEEK OUT WHAT *ALL* SITH SEEK --

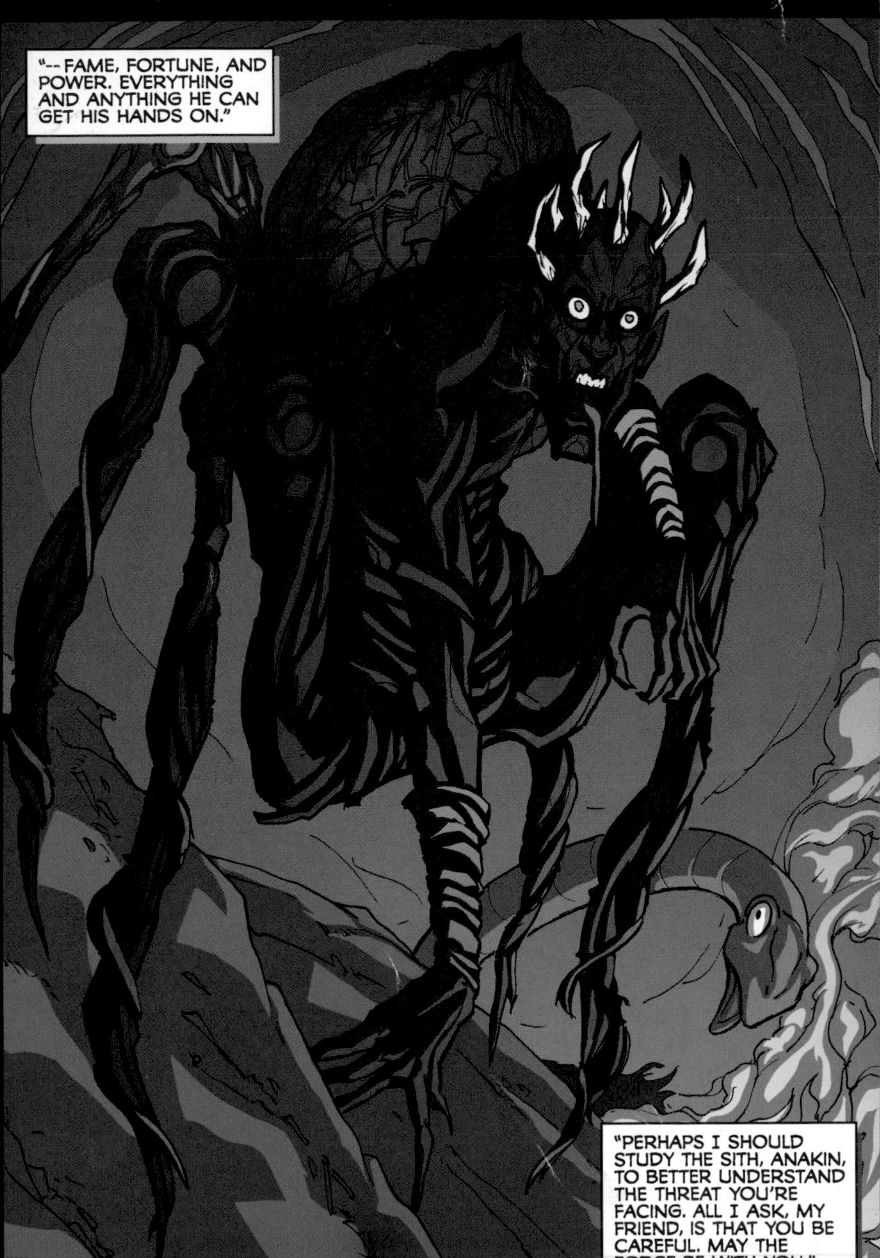
"--FAME, FORTUNE, AND POWER. EVERYTHING AND ANYTHING HE CAN GET HIS HANDS ON."
"PERHAPS I SHOULD STUDY THE SITH, ANAKIN, TO BETTER UNDERSTAND THE THREAT YOU'RE FACING. ALL I ASK, MY FRIEND, IS THAT YOU BE CAREFUL. MAY THE FORCE BE WITH YOU."

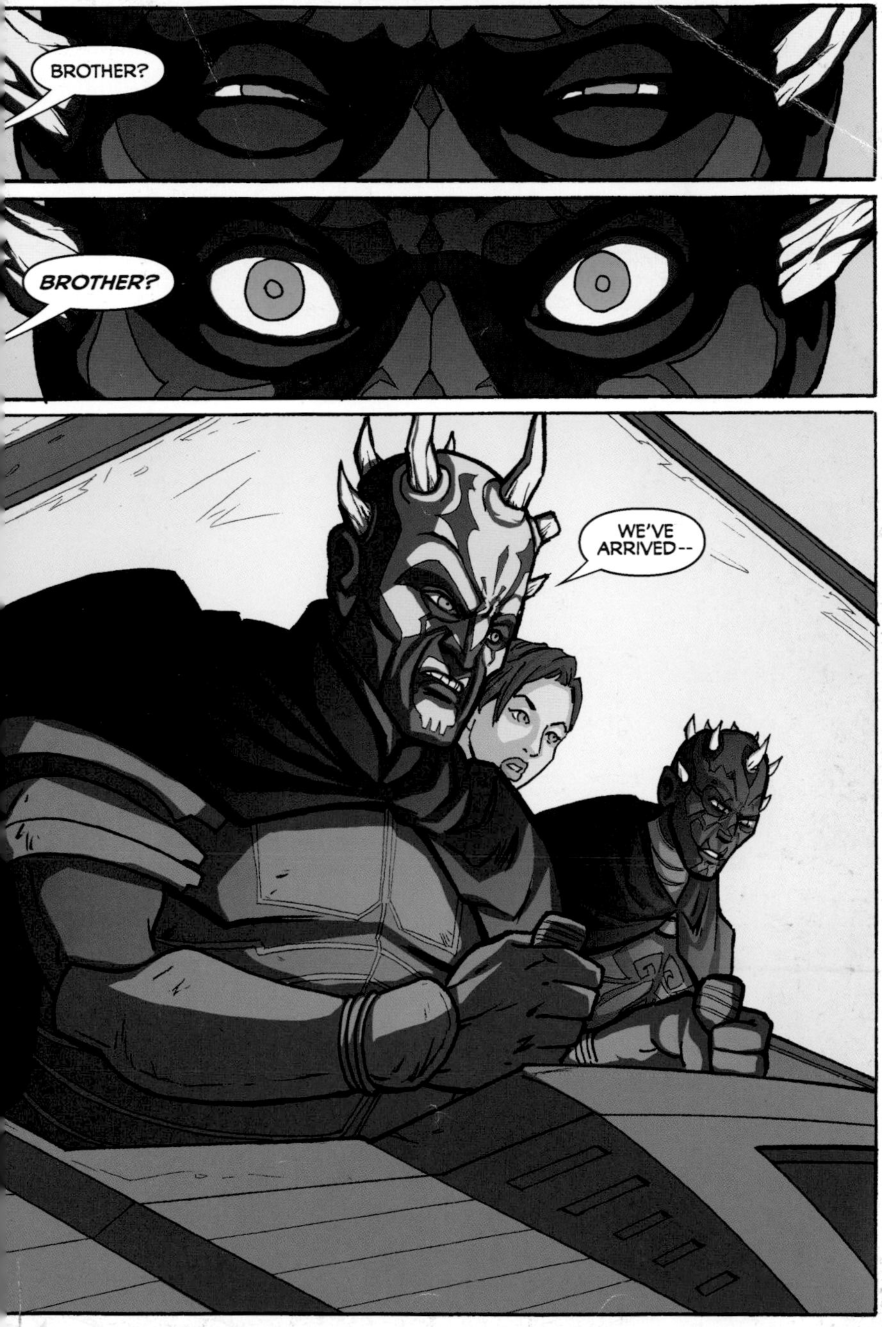
BROTHER?
BROTHER?
WE'VE ARRIVED--

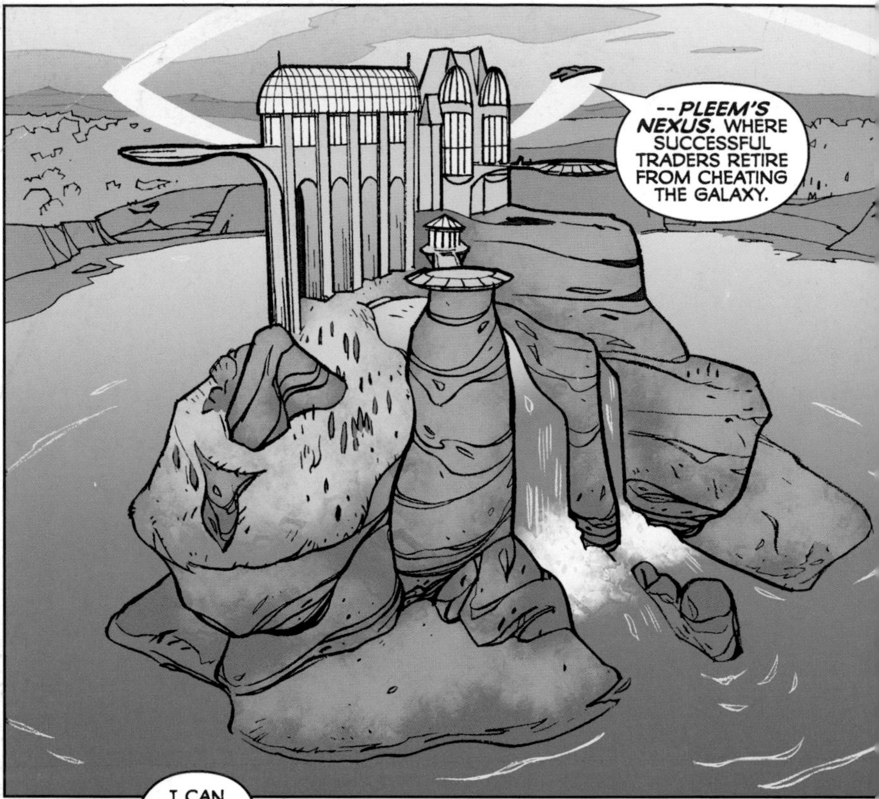
--PLEEM'S NEXUS. WHERE SUCCESSFUL TRADERS RETIRE FROM CHEATING THE GALAXY.

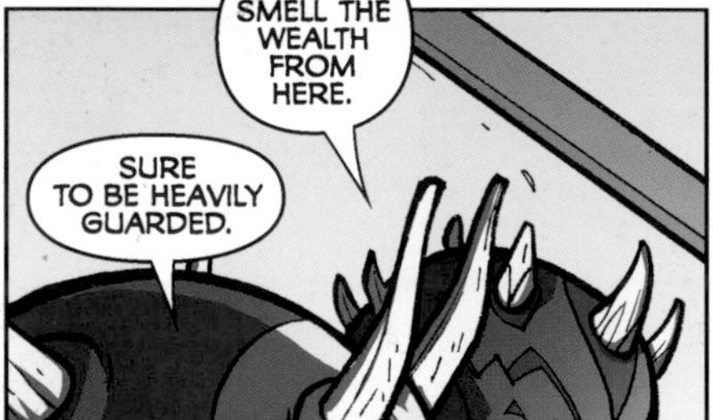
I CAN SMELL THE WEALTH FROM HERE.
SURE TO BE HEAVILY GUARDED.

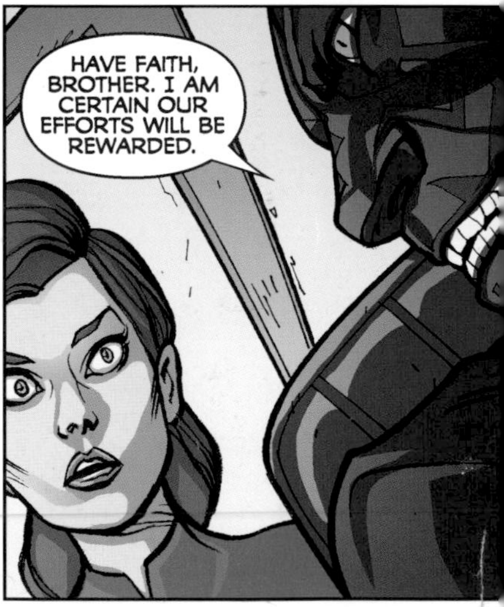
HAVE FAITH, BROTHER. I AM CERTAIN OUR EFFORTS WILL BE REWARDED.

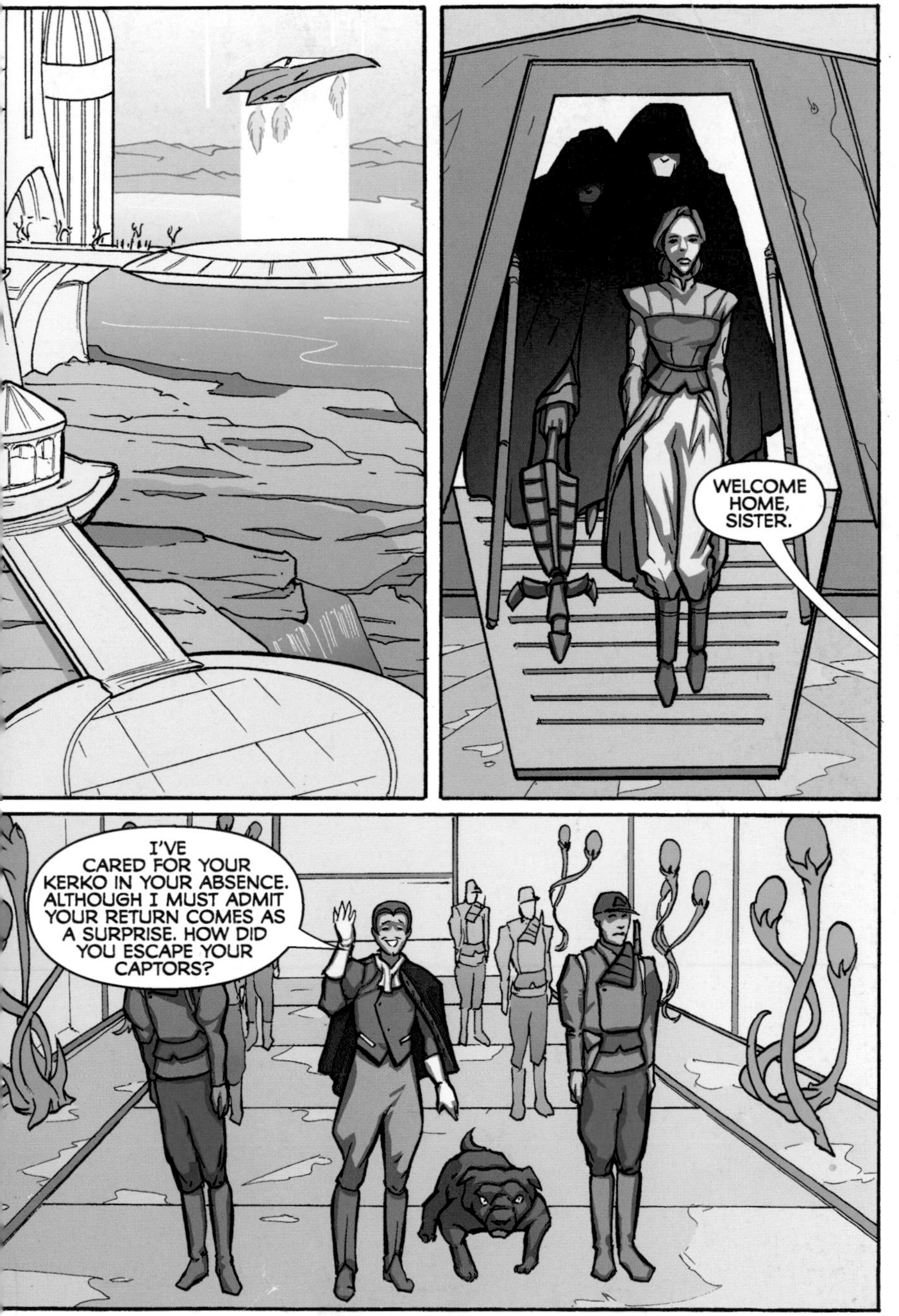
WELCOME HOME, SISTER.
I'VE CARED FOR YOUR KERKO IN YOUR ABSENCE. ALTHOUGH I MUST ADMIT YOUR RETURN COMES AS A SURPRISE. HOW DID YOU ESCAPE YOUR CAPTORS?

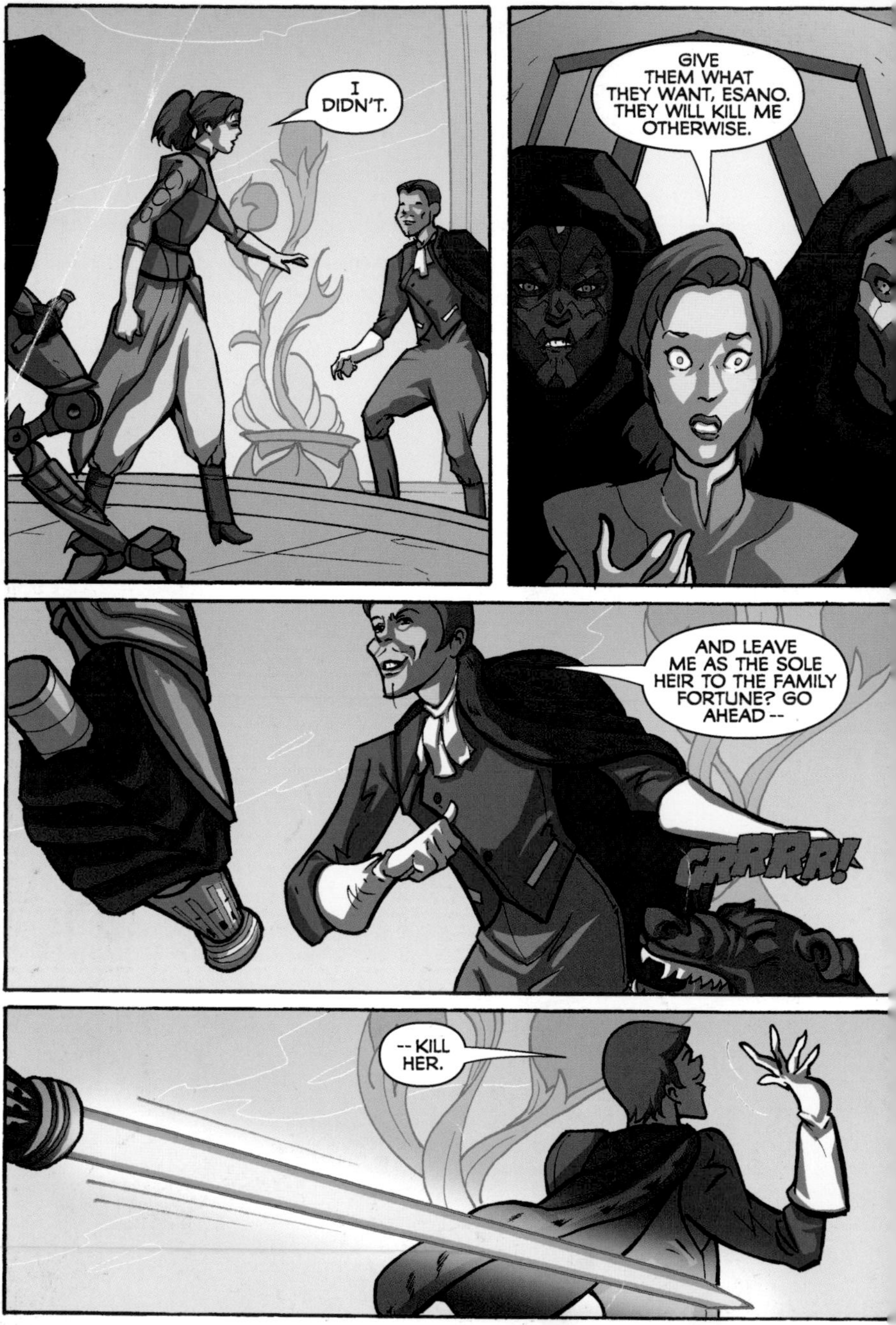
I DIDN'T.
GIVE THEM WHAT THEY WANT, ESANO. THEY WILL KILL ME OTHERWISE.
AND LEAVE ME AS THE SOLE HEIR TO THE FAMILY FORTUNE? GO AHEAD--
GRRRR!
--KILL HER.

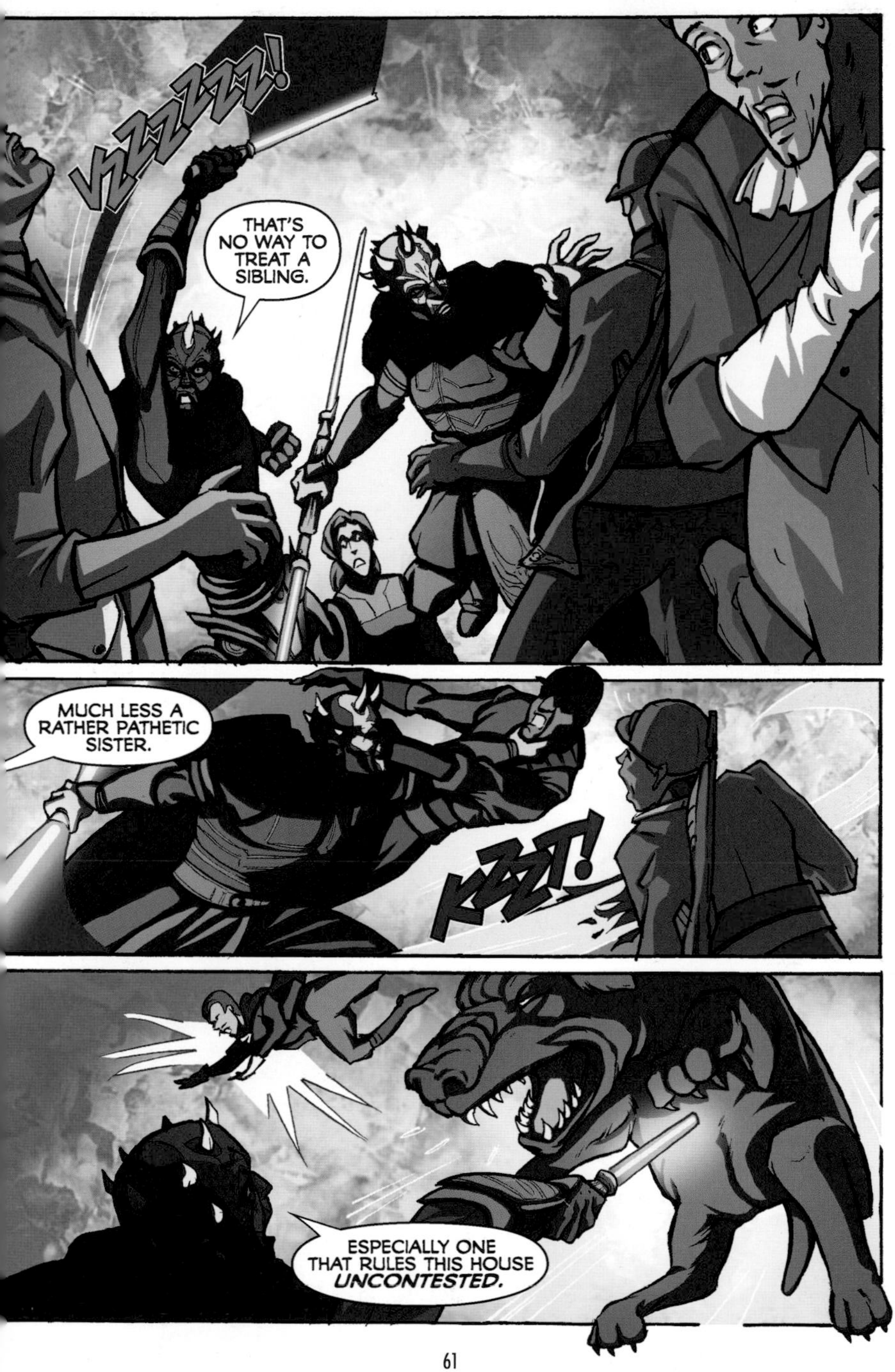
VZZZZZZZ!
THAT'S NO WAY TO TREAT A SIBLING.
MUCH LESS A RATHER PATHETIC SISTER.
KZZZT!
ESPECIALLY ONE THAT RULES THIS HOUSE *UNCONTESTED.*

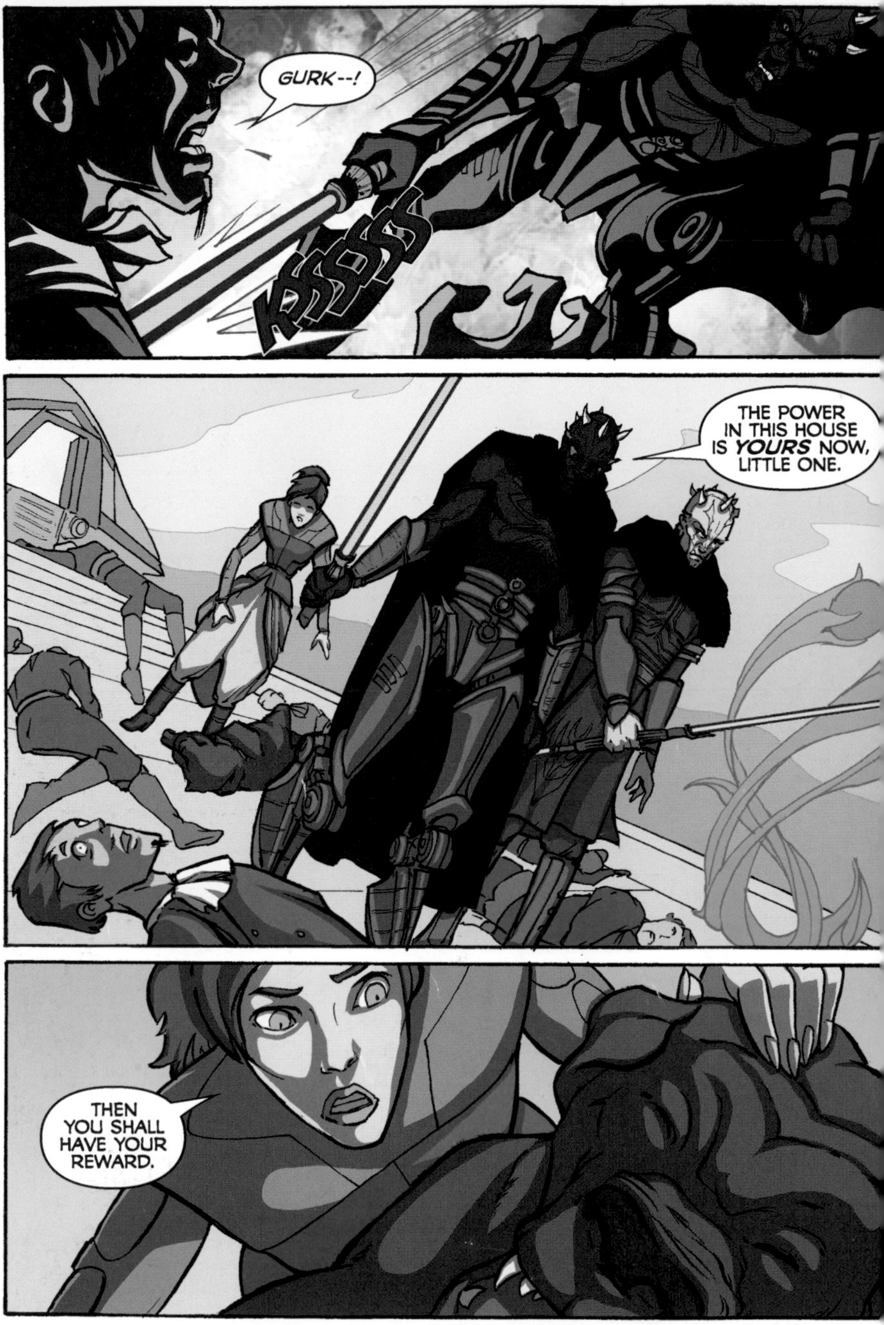
GURK--!
KRSSSSSS
THE POWER IN THIS HOUSE IS *YOURS* NOW, LITTLE ONE.
THEN YOU SHALL HAVE YOUR REWARD.

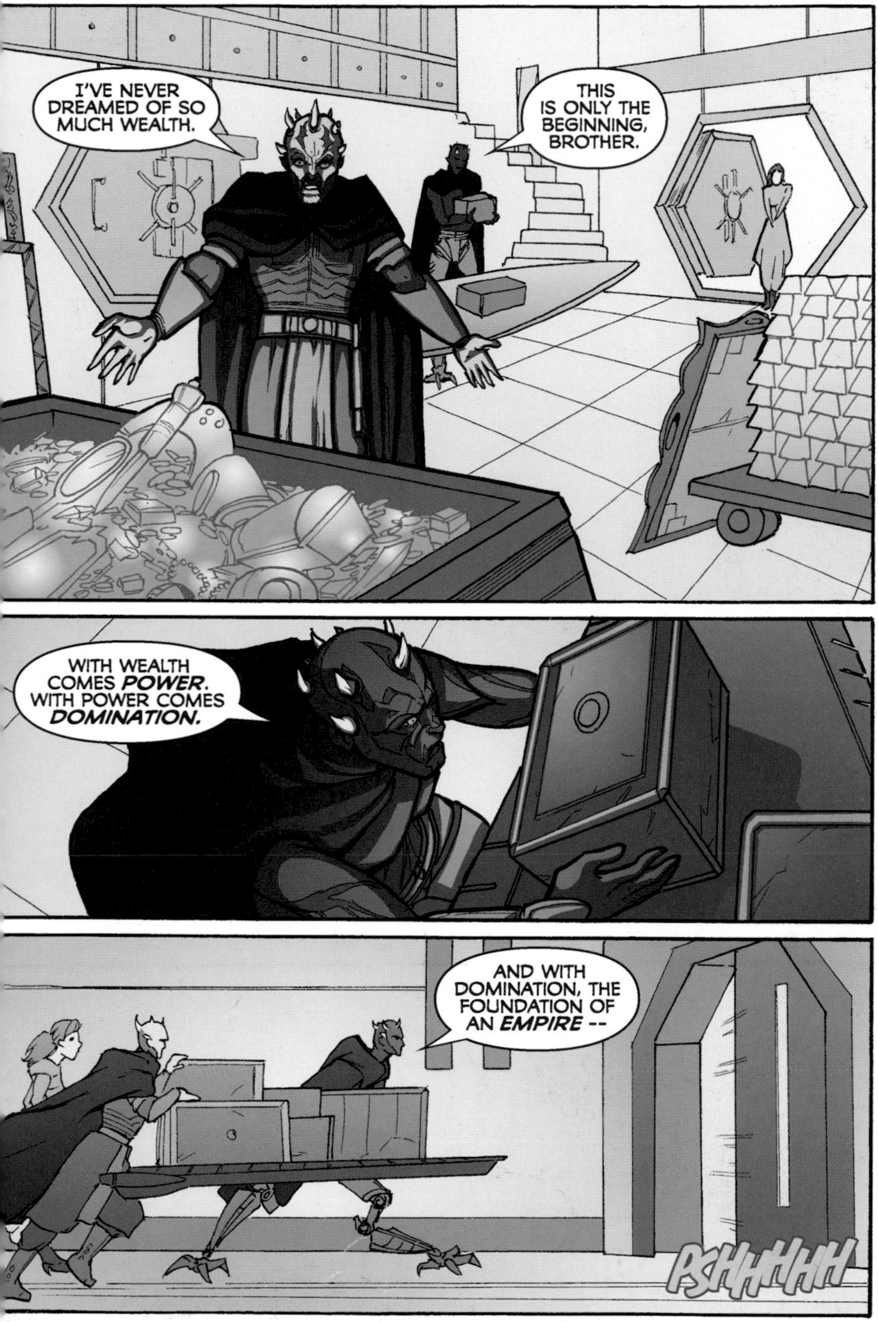

I'VE NEVER DREAMED OF SO MUCH WEALTH.
THIS IS ONLY THE BEGINNING, BROTHER.
WITH WEALTH COMES ***POWER***. WITH POWER COMES ***DOMINATION.***
AND WITH DOMINATION, THE FOUNDATION OF AN ***EMPIRE*** --
PSHHHHHH

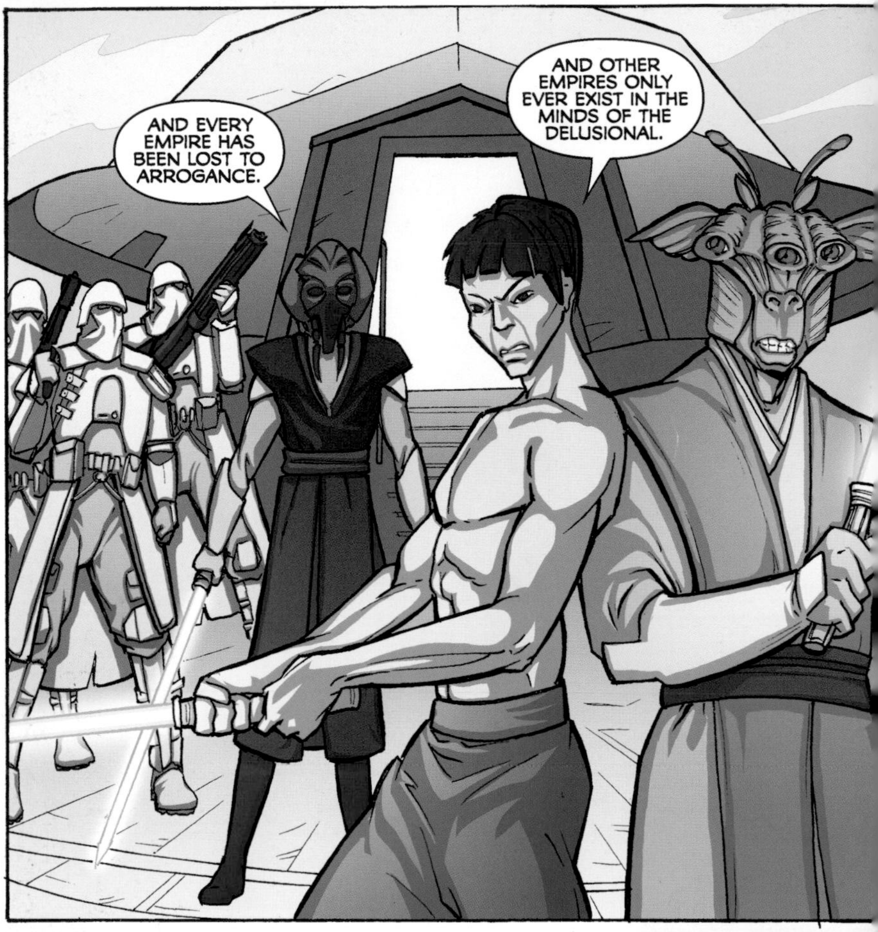
AND EVERY EMPIRE HAS BEEN LOST TO ARROGANCE.
AND OTHER EMPIRES ONLY EVER EXIST IN THE MINDS OF THE DELUSIONAL.

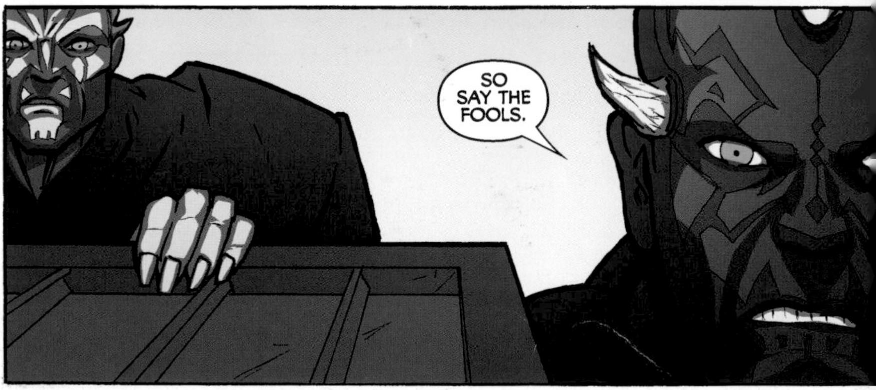
SO SAY THE FOOLS.

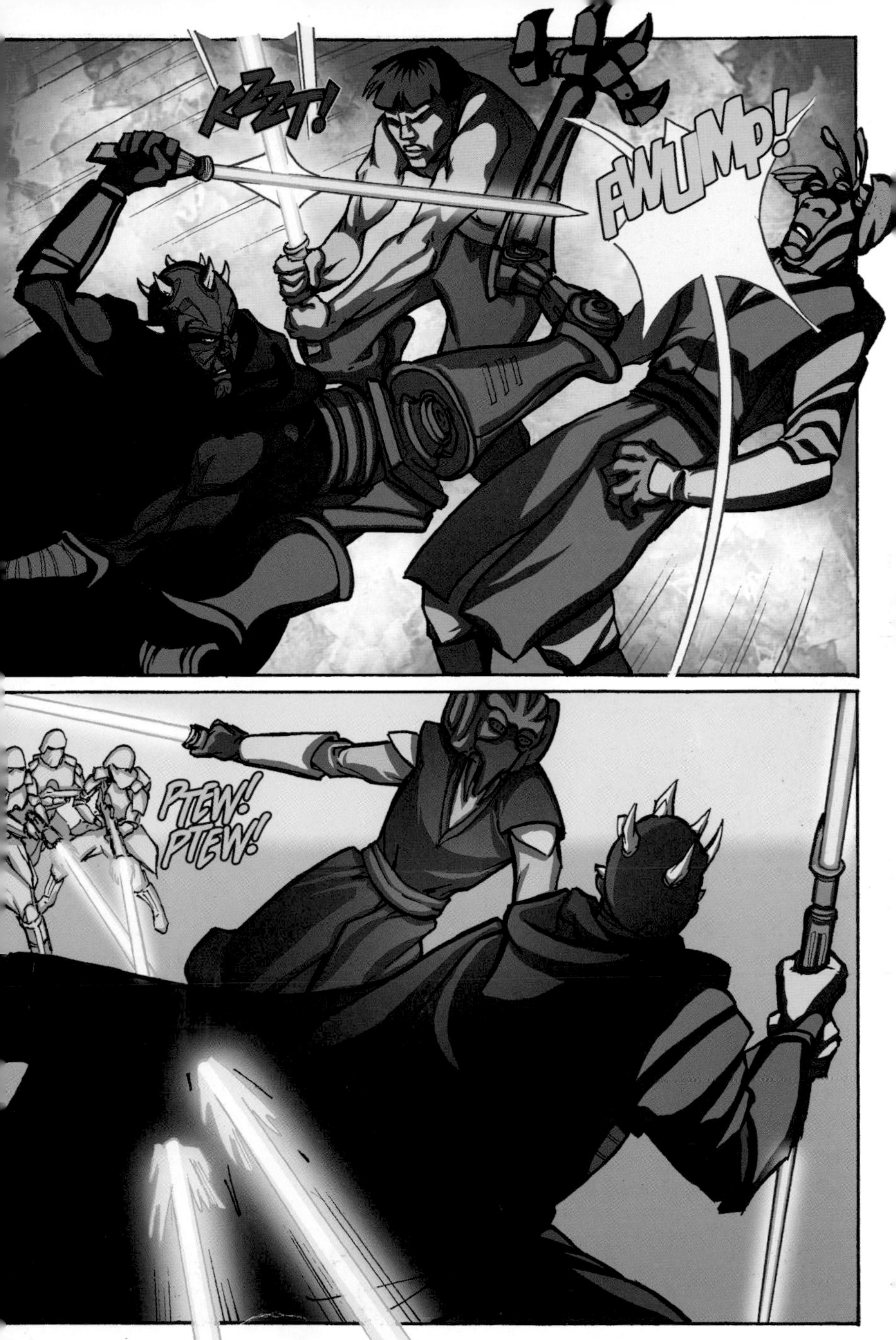
KZZT!
FWUMP!
PTEW!
PTEW!

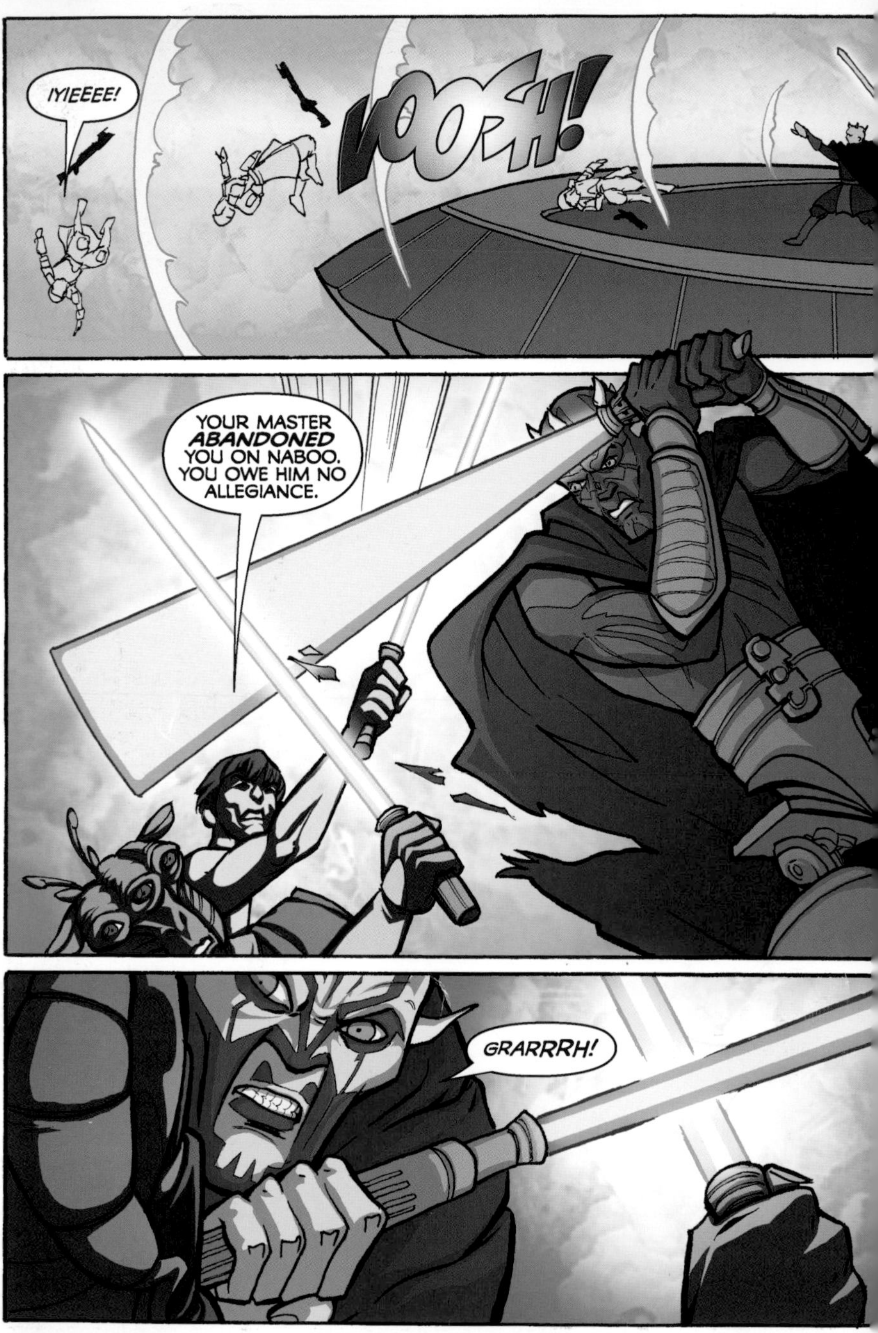
IYIEEEE!
VOOSH!
YOUR MASTER ABANDONED YOU ON NABOO. YOU OWE HIM NO ALLEGIANCE.
GRARRRH!

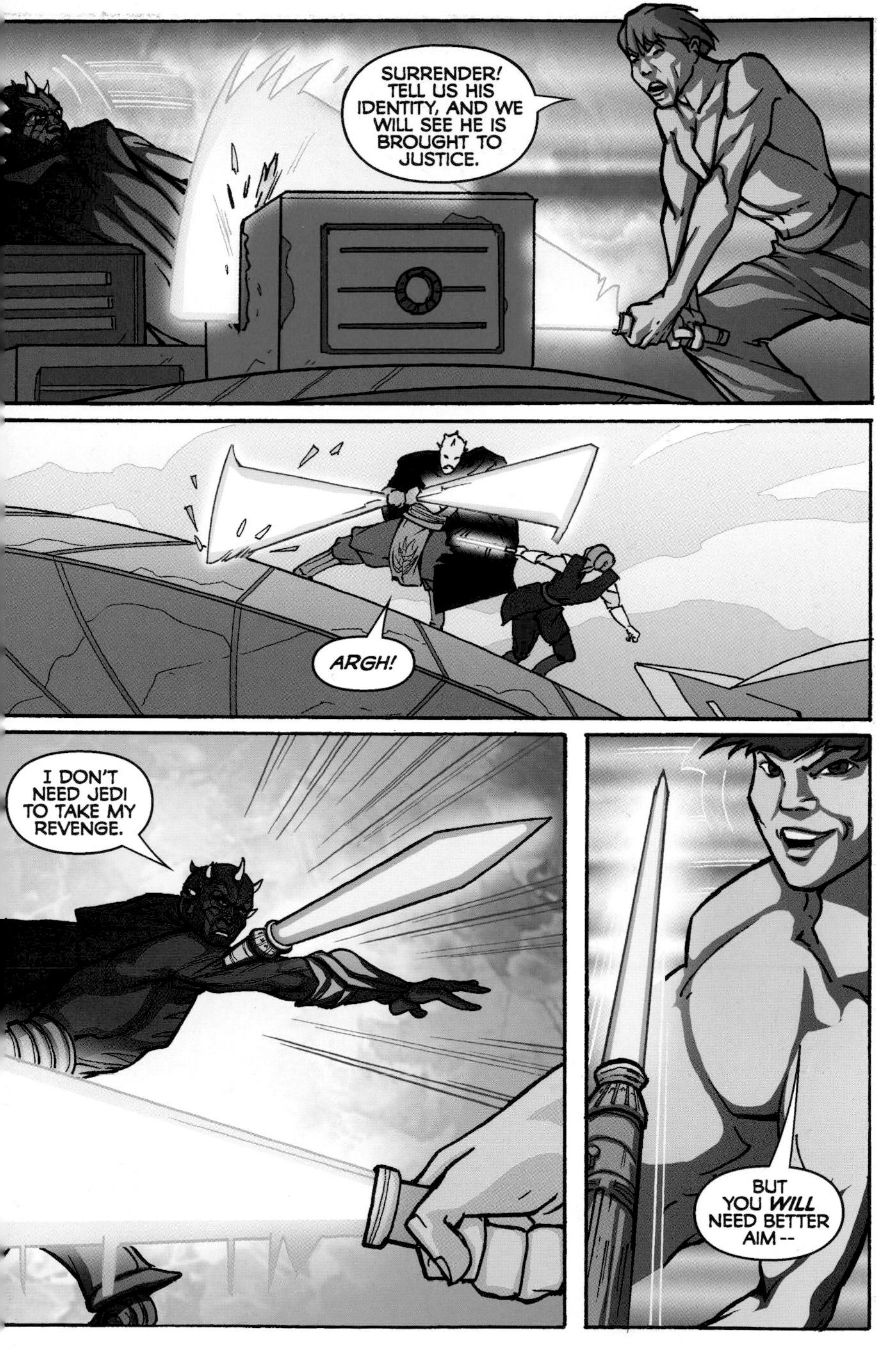
SURRENDER! TELL US HIS IDENTITY, AND WE WILL SEE HE IS BROUGHT TO JUSTICE.
ARGH!
I DON'T NEED JEDI TO TAKE MY REVENGE.
BUT YOU WILL NEED BETTER AIM --

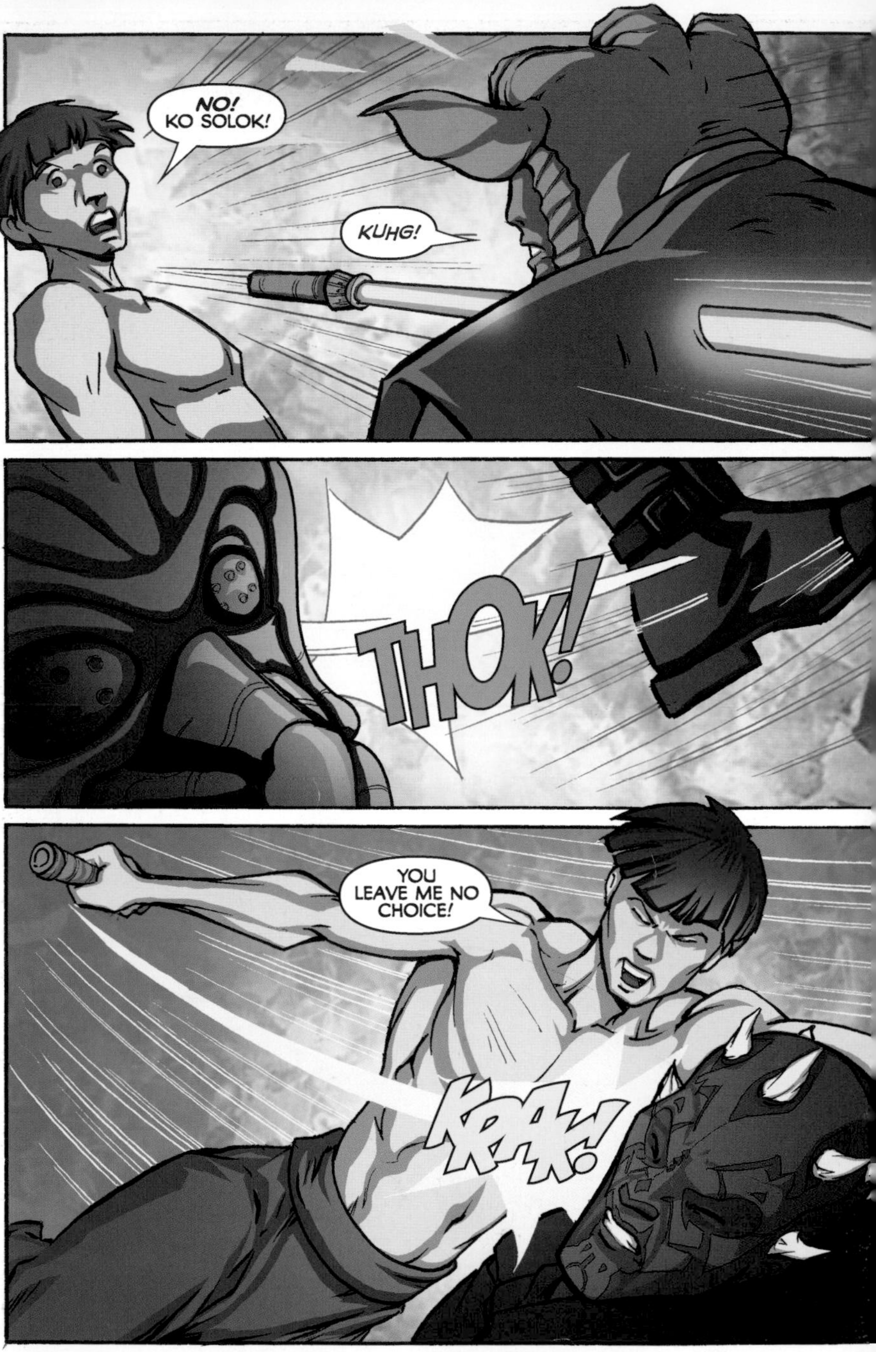
NO! KO SOLOK!
KUHG!
THOK!
YOU LEAVE ME NO CHOICE!
KRAK!

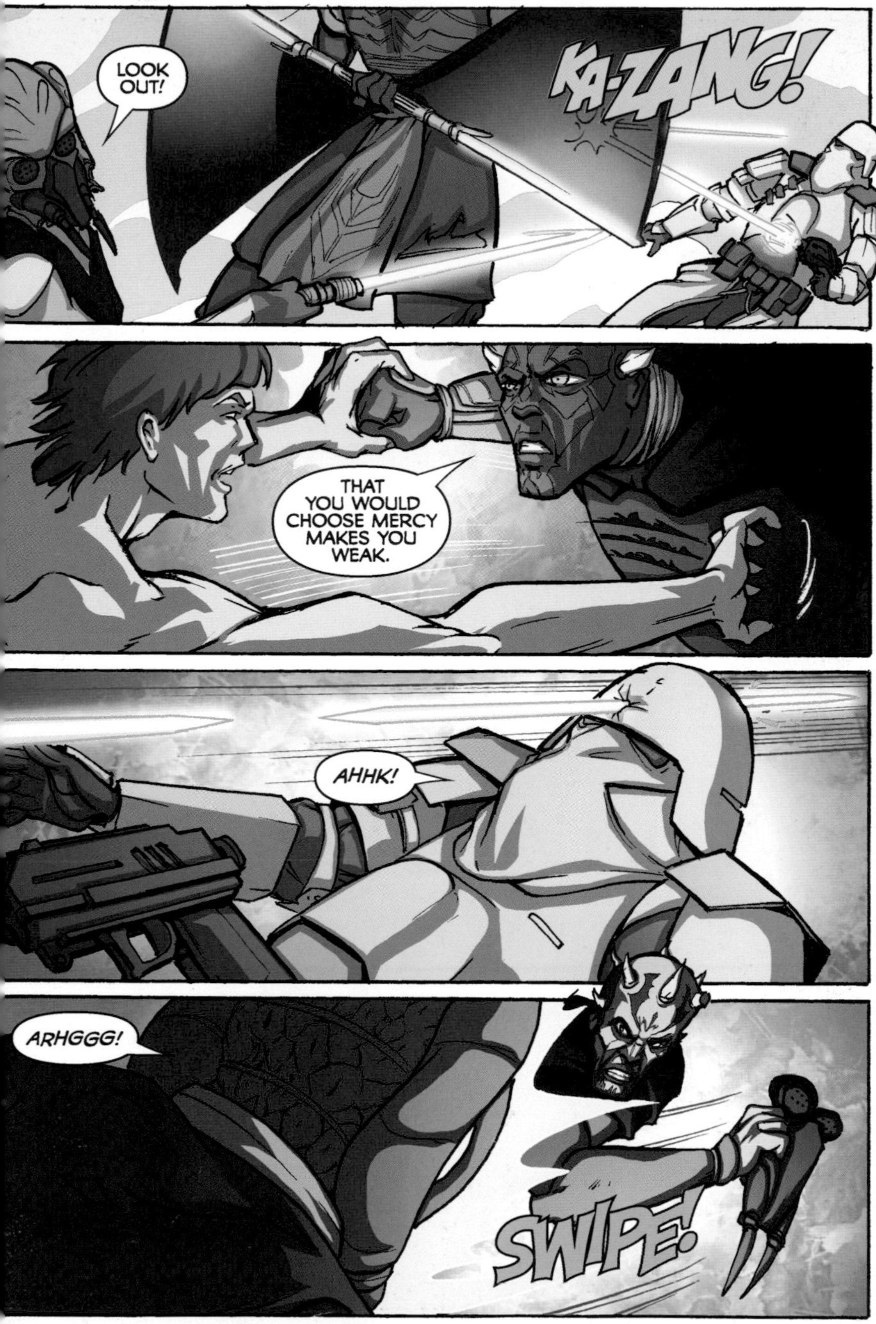
LOOK OUT!
KA-ZANG!
THAT YOU WOULD CHOOSE MERCY MAKES YOU WEAK.
AHHK!
ARHGGG!
SWIPE!

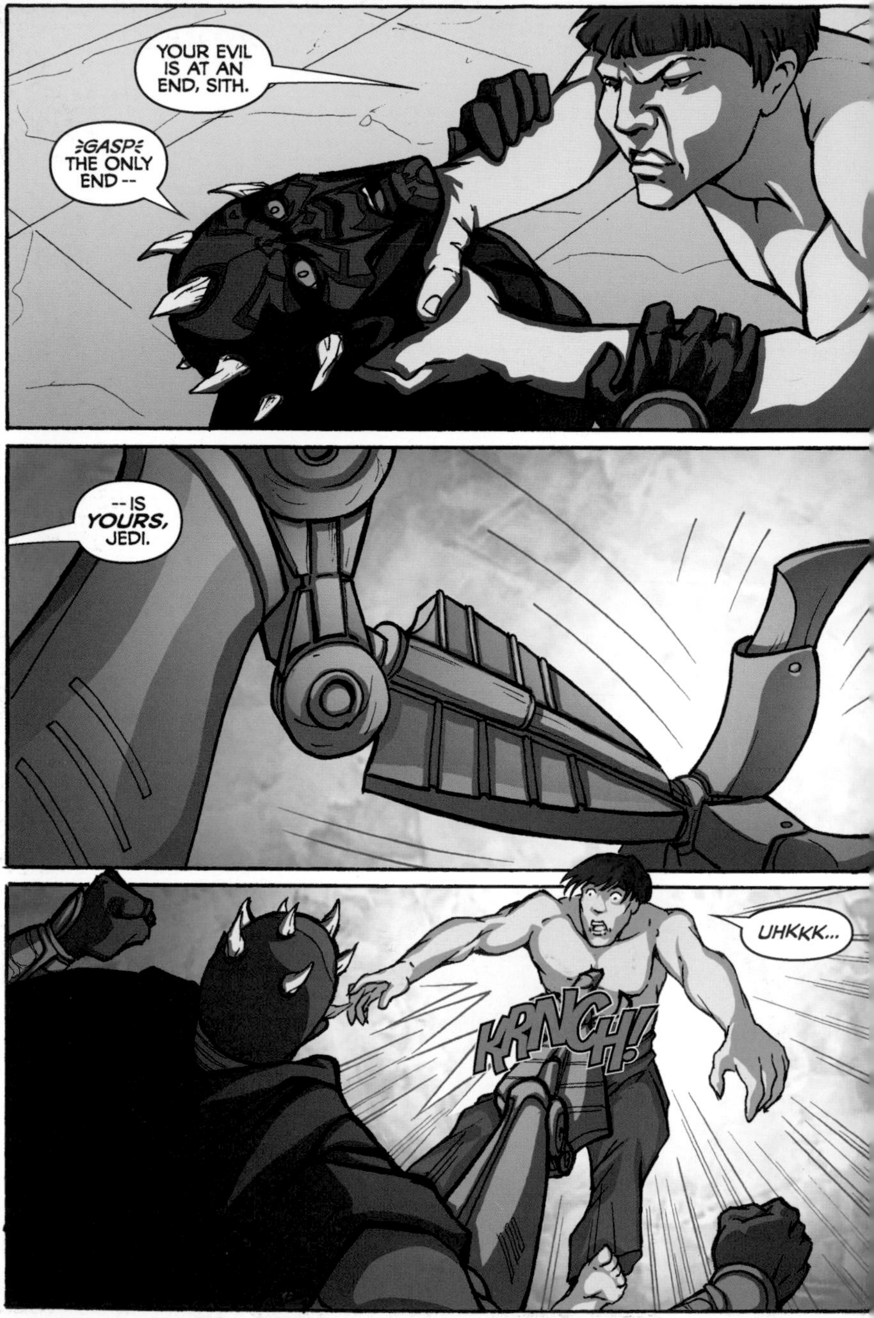
YOUR EVIL IS AT AN END, SITH.
GASP THE ONLY END --
-- IS YOURS, JEDI.
UHKKK...
KRNCH!

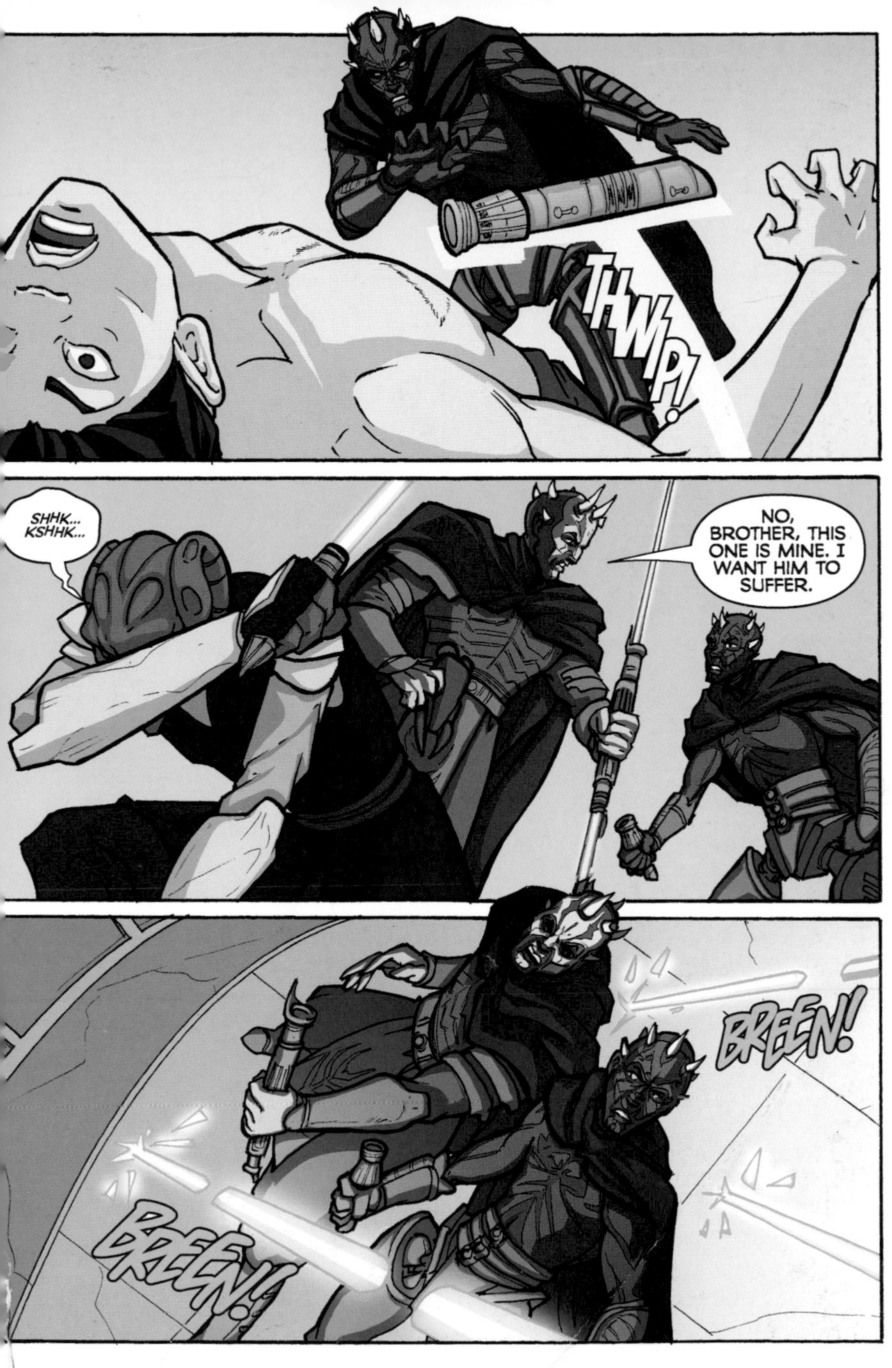
THWIP!
SHHK... KSHHK...
NO, BROTHER, THIS ONE IS MINE. I WANT HIM TO SUFFER.
BREEN!
BREEN!

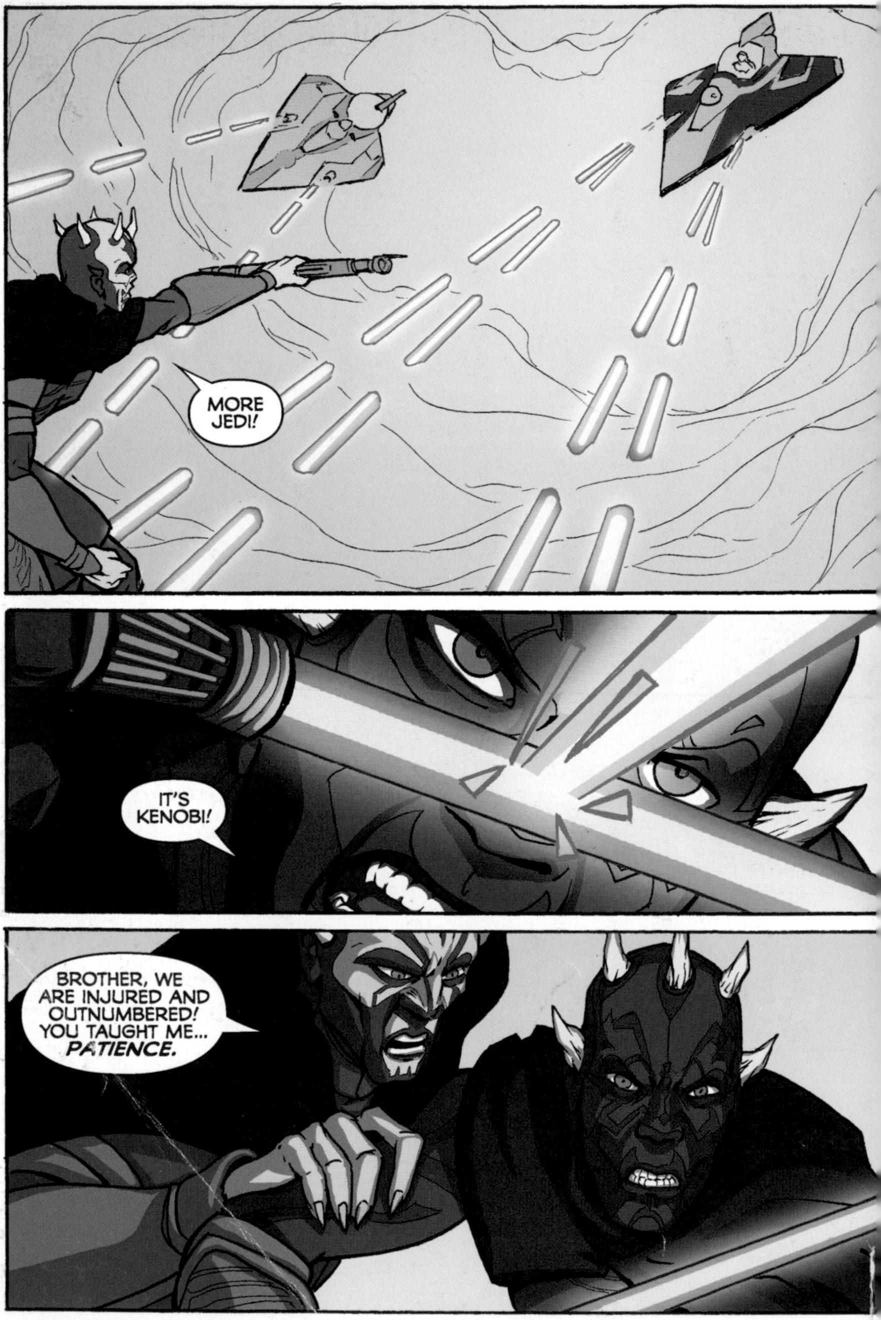
MORE JEDI!
IT'S KENOBI!
BROTHER, WE ARE INJURED AND OUTNUMBERED! YOU TAUGHT ME... PATIENCE.

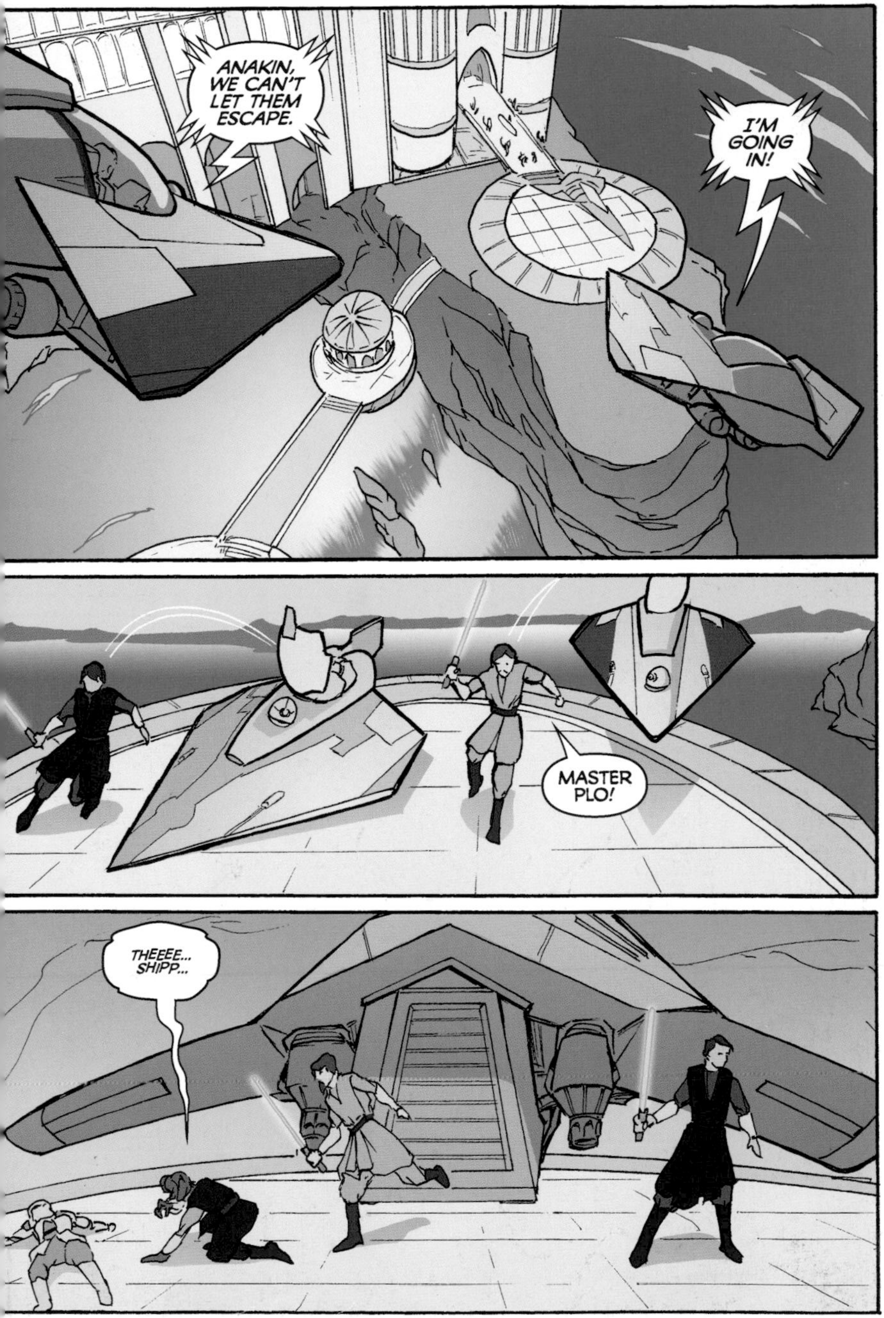
ANAKIN, WE CAN'T LET THEM ESCAPE.
I'M GOING IN!
MASTER PLO!
THEEEE... SHIPP...

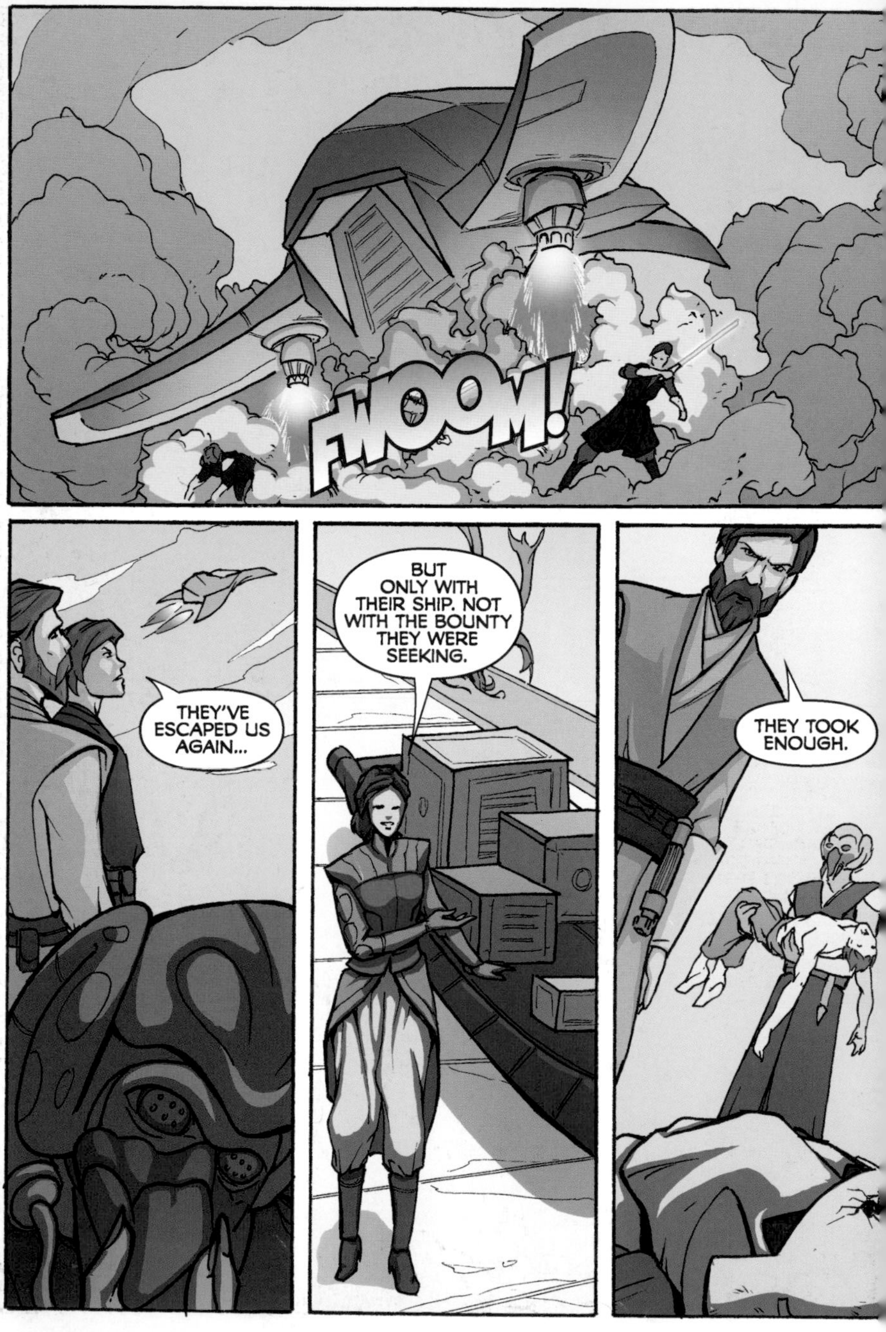
FWOOM!
THEY'VE ESCAPED US AGAIN...
BUT ONLY WITH THEIR SHIP. NOT WITH THE BOUNTY THEY WERE SEEKING.
THEY TOOK ENOUGH.

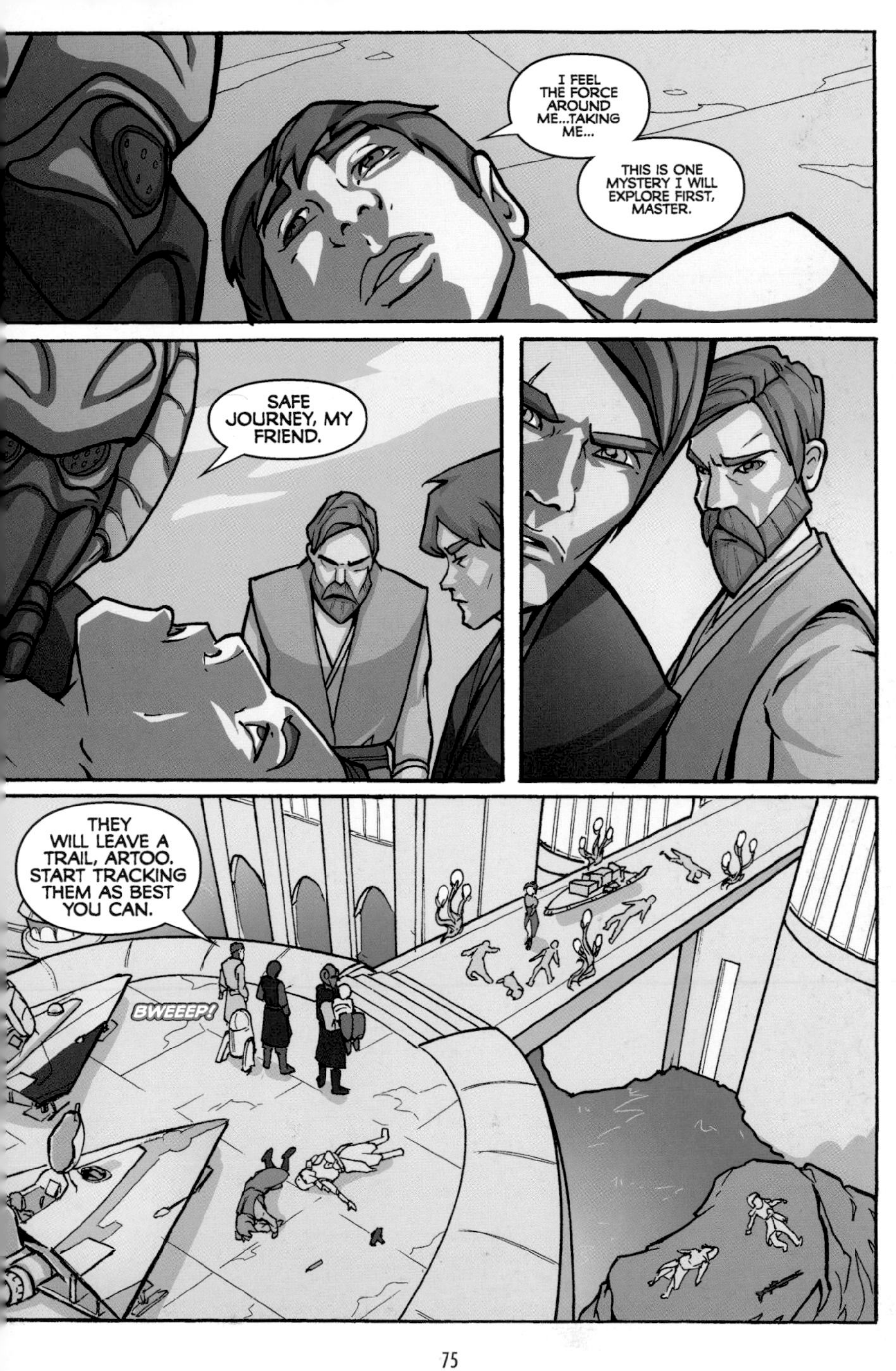
I FEEL THE FORCE AROUND ME...TAKING ME...
THIS IS ONE MYSTERY I WILL EXPLORE FIRST, MASTER.
SAFE JOURNEY, MY FRIEND.
THEY WILL LEAVE A TRAIL, ARTOO. START TRACKING THEM AS BEST YOU CAN.
BWEEEP!

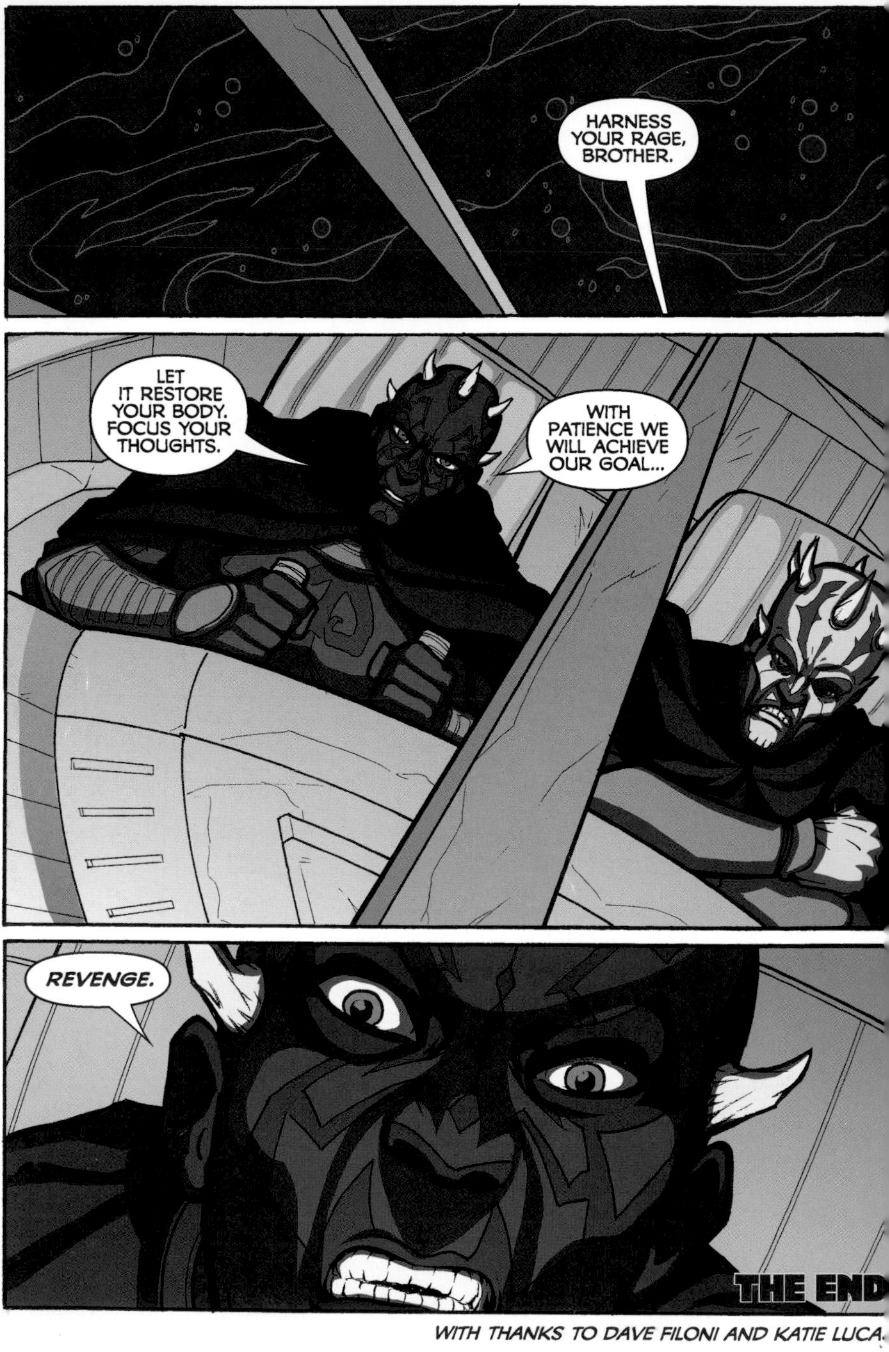
HARNESS YOUR RAGE, BROTHER.
LET IT RESTORE YOUR BODY. FOCUS YOUR THOUGHTS.
WITH PATIENCE WE WILL ACHIEVE OUR GOAL...
REVENGE.
THE END

WITH THANKS TO DAVE FILONI AND KATIE LUCA.

PRESIDENT AND PUBLISHER **MIKE RICHARDSON**

EXECUTIVE VICE PRESIDENT **NEIL HANKERSON**

CHIEF FINANCIAL OFFICER **TOM WEDDLE**

VICE PRESIDENT OF PUBLISHING **RANDY STRADLEY**

VICE PRESIDENT OF BOOK TRADE SALES **MICHAEL MARTENS**

VICE PRESIDENT OF BUSINESS AFFAIRS **ANITA NELSON**

VICE PRESIDENT OF PRODUCT DEVELOPMENT **DAVID SCROGGY**

VICE PRESIDENT OF INFORMATION TECHNOLOGY **DALE LAFOUNTAIN**

SENIOR DIRECTOR OF PRINT, DESIGN, AND PRODUCTION **DARLENE VOGEL**

GENERAL COUNSEL **KEN LIZZI**

SENIOR DIRECTOR OF MARKETING **MATT PARKINSON**

EDITORIAL DIRECTOR **DAVEY ESTRADA**

SENIOR MANAGING EDITOR **SCOTT ALLIE**

SENIOR BOOKS EDITOR **CHRIS WARNER**

EXECUTIVE EDITOR **DIANA SCHUTZ**

DIRECTOR OF PRINT AND DEVELOPMENT **CARY GRAZZINI**

ART DIRECTOR **LIA RIBACCHI**

DIRECTOR OF SCHEDULING **CARA NIECE**

STAR WARS GRAPHIC NOVEL TIMELINE (IN YEARS

Omnibus: Tales of the Jedi—5,000–3,986 BSW4

Knights of the Old Republic—3,964–3,963 BSW4

The Old Republic—3653, 3678 BSW4

Knight Errant—1,032 BSW4

Jedi vs. Sith—1,000 BSW4

Omnibus: Rise of the Sith—33 BSW4

Episode I: The Phantom Menace—32 BSW4

Omnibus: Emissaries and Assassins—32 BSW4

Omnibus: Quinlan Vos—Jedi in Darkness—31–30 BSW4

Omnibus: Menace Revealed—31–22 BSW4

Honor and Duty—22 BSW4

Blood Ties—22 BSW4

Episode II: Attack of the Clones—22 BSW4

Clone Wars—22–19 BSW4

Clone Wars Adventures—22–19 BSW4

General Grievous—22–19 BSW4

Episode III: Revenge of the Sith—19 BSW4

Dark Times—19 BSW4

Omnibus: Droids—5.5 BSW4

Omnibus: Boba Fett—3 BSW4–10 ASW4

Omnibus: At War with the Empire—1 BSW4

Episode IV: A New Hope—SW4

Classic Star Wars—0–3 ASW4

Omnibus: A Long Time Ago . . .—0–4 ASW4

Empire—0 ASW4

Omnibus: The Other Sons of Tatooine—0 ASW4

Omnibus: Early Victories—0–3 ASW4

Jabba the Hutt: The Art of the Deal—1 ASW4

Episode V: The Empire Strikes Back—3 ASW4

Omnibus: Shadows of the Empire—3.5–4.5 ASW4

Episode VI: Return of the Jedi—4 ASW4

Omnibus: X-Wing Rogue Squadron—4–5 ASW4

Heir to the Empire—9 ASW4

Dark Force Rising—9 ASW4

The Last Command—9 ASW4

Dark Empire—10 ASW4

Crimson Empire—11 ASW4

Jedi Academy: Leviathan—12 ASW4

Union—19 ASW4

Chewbacca—25 ASW4

Invasion—25 ASW4

Legacy—130–137 ASW4

Old Republic Era
25,000 – 1000 years before
Star Wars: A New Hope

Rise of the Empire Era
1000 – 0 years before
Star Wars: A New Hope

Rebellion Era
0 – 5 years after
Star Wars: A New Hope

New Republic Era
5 – 25 years after
Star Wars: A New Hope

New Jedi Order Era
25+ years after
Star Wars: A New Hope

Legacy Era
130+ years after
Star Wars: A New Hope

Vector
Crosses four eras in the timeline

Volume 1 contains:
Knights of the Old Republic Volume 5
Dark Times Volume 3

Volume 2 contains:
Rebellion Volume 4
Legacy Volume 6

BSW4 = before *Episode IV: A New Hope*. ASW4 = after *Episode IV: A New Hope*.